FIGURE SKATING NOW

OLYMPIC AND WORLD STARS

SECOND EDITION

FIGURE SKATING NOW

OLYMPIC AND WORLD STARS

Gérard Châtaigneau & Steve Milton

FIREFLY BOOKS

A FIREFLY BOOK

Published by Firefly Books Ltd. 2003

First Printing

National Library of Canada Cataloguing in Publication Data

Milton, Steve
    Figure skating now : Olympic and world champions / by Steve Milton ;
photography by Gérard Châtaigneau. -- 2nd ed.

ISBN 1-55297-833-8
1. Skaters–Biography. 2. Skating. I. Châtaigneau, Gérard II. Title.
GV850.A2M54 2003   796.91'2'0922   C2003-903970-6

Publisher Cataloging-in-Publication Data (U.S)
(Library of Congress Standards)

Milton, Steve.
    Figure skating now : Olympic and world stars/ Steve Milton ;
Gérard Châtaigneau._2nd ed.

[128] p. : col. photos. ; cm.

Summary: Biographies and photographs of contemporary figure skating champions.
ISBN 1-55297-833-8 (pbk.)

1. Skaters–Biography. 2. Skating–Pictorial works. I. Châtaigneau, Gérard. III. Title.
796.91/2/0922 B 21   GV850.A2M55 2003

Published in Canada in 2003 by
Firefly Books Ltd.
3680 Victoria Park Avenue
Toronto, Ontario, Canada   M2H 3K1

Published in the United States in 2003 by
Firefly Books (U.S.) Inc.
P.O. Box 1338, Ellicott Station
Buffalo, New York, USA   14205

Design by Interrobang Graphic Design Inc.
Printed and bound in Canada by Friesens, Altona, Manitoba

*The Publisher acknowledges the financial support of the Government of Canada through
the Book Publishing Industry Development Program for its publishing activities.*

CONTENTS

INTRODUCTION

Extraordinary people create extraordinary moments.

Michelle Kwan is likely the most extraordinary women's figure skating champion of all time. Her championships, both at the 2003 U.S. Nationals and at Worlds the same year, will be remembered as inspired, captivating and perfect in delivery and technique. Meanwhile, Shae-Lynn Bourne and Victor Kraatz, Canada's ice dance champions, have joined a long list of Canadian heroes in claiming the first-ever world title in ice dance – not just for Canada, but for North America. So now there are more nations competing for top honors in ice dancing.

These are times for greatness. They are trying times, too, for figure skating is dealing with new scoring systems, new structures and new challenges. But in the midst of turmoil, great skating still shines. And the list of talented skaters sparkles with new names.

In the ladies' event, the United States is showing enormous strength. Jennifer Kirk and Ann-Patrice McDonough are some of the new stars who will gain more international exposure. They will join the breathtakingly talented Sasha Cohen who, with only one year of Grand Prix competitions behind her, has already established herself as a leading force within the new generation. And what about Olympic gold medalist Sarah Hughes? Will she continue to compete and go on to reach new heights? Or is her decision to attend Yale the practical end to a mercurial career?

Fumie Suguri, Shizuka Arakawa and Yoshie Onda, all exuding a blend of grace and power, have established Japan as a solid contender in ladies' skating. Fumie delights us with her sophisticated and balletic style. Shizuka, the "one gold blade" skating marvel, has a more contemporary approach. And Yoshie is gentle, yet all powerful with intense determination. Add some Russian gusto into the mix, and you can be sure that the ladies'

figure skating scene will continue to thrill us for some time to come.

Ice dancing is, in short, a whole new world. Shae-Lynn Bourne and Victor Kraatz have provided the inspiration, as great teams from the United States and Canada press forward with credible challenges. Europe has always provided superb dancers, but who would have expected Bulgaria to make headlines? Yet that is what the innovative Albena Denkova and Maxim Staviyski have achieved for their country.

In pairs, China has emerged as the new powerhouse. It fielded three teams in the 2003 Worlds. Xue Shen and Hongbo Zhao skated to a gold medal, and the other teams placed a more than respectable fourth and sixth. Russia is also very strong in this discipline with, notably, Tatiana Totmianina and Maxim Marinin. It will be interesting not only to watch the Chinese–Russian contest, but also to see which countries will develop new teams.

If inspiration and drive come from example, then the new names in men's figure skating need only to look at the one man who made the quad a necessary weapon – because he's back! Elvis Stojko has returned to competition, and that says plenty. Yes, the quad is no longer a novelty, it's a necessity and, like the triple Axel before it, has become the dividing line between good skaters and top skaters. It's almost impossible now to win a medal without two quad jumps, one of which will be combined with a triple. With skaters from the United States, Russia, France, Japan and China trying to cram into the final flight, the men's event has become truly international.

So with all these extraordinary developments, how does one push the envelope these days? I'm not even going to take a guess. What lies ahead is unpredictable. Just watch. And be amazed.

Gérard Châtaigneau

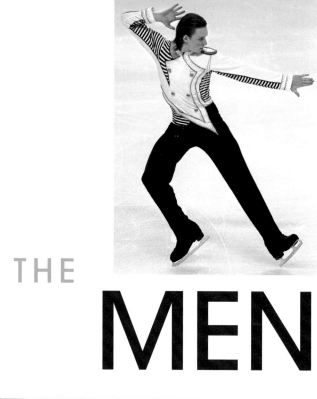

THE MEN

Evgeny Plushenko

Alexei Yagudin

Timothy Goebel

Takeshi Honda

Michael Weiss

Chengjiang Li

Emanuel Sandhu

Ilia Klimkin

Brian Joubert

Jeff Buttle

Ryan Jahnke

Alexander Abt

Stanick Jeannette

No sport has jumped forward so quickly as men's figure skating has. And this comes from guys who spend most of their time facing backward. Kurt Browning, the man who landed the world's first quadruple jump in 1988, didn't even need to do one to win his four world titles before turning pro in 1994. Even as late as December 1997 at the Grand Prix Final in Hamilton, Ontario, for the first

time there was a total of three quads landed by the same flight of skaters. One of them was Elvis Stojko's quad-triple, the first in skating history.

But by 1999, American Tim Goebel had landed three quads by himself in the same program. In 2001, new world champion Evgeny Plushenko raised the bar with a quad-triple-double combination, which inspired other elite skaters to frantically practice the nine-rotation set during the off-season. At 2001 Worlds, just 39 months after Stojko unleashed the first quad-triple combination, there were five of them landed in the short program, and six more in the freeskate. And many, many others were attempted. Plushenko and Tim Goebel were also predicting that they would eventually do all six recognized jumps as quadruples.

"With the jumping and improved presentation," says Alexei Yagudin, "you really, really have to work to be in the top group." Yagudin's done a pretty good job of that, winning three straight Worlds before finishing second to Plushenko's magnificent performance in 2001. But despite his spectacular record when it counted most, Yagudin didn't always dominate during the season, emphasizing just how deep the men's field has become. Additionally, the roster is no longer divided into jumpers and artists. Plushenko is one of the most captivating performers in the sport, with interesting spins and long lines, and is also one of the best jumpers. Canadian Emanuel Sandhu, a throwback to a more balletic era, has become a sudden challenger by perfecting his quad-triple. Japan's Yamato Tamura is so electrifying, he has a rock-star appeal in his home country.

More purely athletic types such as Yagudin, Stojko and Michael Weiss have matured and found perfect

choreographic vehicles, most often in blockbuster-movie themes. Many of those who find themselves just out of reach of the podium do so because their presentation, not their athleticism, is still developing. "You have got to have the whole package now to win this thing," says prominent coach Doug Leigh. Still, Todd Eldredge won a bronze medal at 2001 Worlds without attempting a quad, and his longtime rival Stojko won a silver the year before when he missed his. They had other strong assets to fall back upon.

Eldredge, at 29, became the oldest skater to win a world medal in 70 years. Stojko was 28 when he won his silver the season before. Many other top-10 contenders are in their 20s, so there is a maturity level in men's skating that didn't exist in the past. That, in turn, has increased the entertainment quotient. But there is also a heavy emphasis on youth. Plushenko and Yagudin won Worlds while still in their teens.

The rivalry between Plushenko and Yagudin is obvious, although both claim it isn't bitter. In any case, the two of them disproved the theory that Russian skating would wither when the Soviet Union collapsed in 1992. If anything, it's become stronger. Including Yagudin and Plushenko, Russian men won four World Juniors titles in six years and four straight Worlds. As Alexander Abt, ranked eighth in the world, can attest, sometimes it's harder to place well at Russian Nationals than at Worlds.

The same could be said for the men's division's fastest-rising country. China's Zhengxin Guo was the first man to land two quads in the same program in 1997; but he finished eighth at 2000 Worlds, and couldn't even make the world team for 2001. Yunfei Li finished only fourth at Chinese Nationals in 2001, but was sixth at Worlds. The winners of the men's Junior Grand Prix Final in 2000 and 2001 were both Chinese. And of the seven quads successfully landed in the short program at 2001 Worlds, three were by the Chinese men and a fourth by Australia's Anthony Liu, who was trained in China. The Chinese moved all their skaters to a training center in Beijing two years before Salt Lake City, to prepare for the Olympics. The Chinese have never won a Worlds in men's – but they're knocking on the door.

It's a very crowded house, however. In fact, Elvis Stojko announced his retirement after the 2002 Olympics, where he finished seventh. But in April 2003, after a season of professional touring, Stojko announced that he would return to eligible skating. The three-time world champion and two-time Olympic silver medalist even intimated that he might stay on the scene until the 2006 Games. Stojko was the one who triggered the quad revolution by landing one in almost every program during the early 1990s, then adding the world's first quad-double and, in 1996, the first quad-triple. But a horrible groin injury suffered in January 1998 affected the final four years of his amateur career. He skated on virtually one leg in the 1998 Olympics and still won a silver medal. After being away from the rigors of amateur competition for a year, Stojko's body – which had not been 100 percent even four years after the injury – felt "right for the first time since the injury." And so, one of the greatest true competitors in skating history announced that he would be back on the international circuit in the 2003–04 season.

All in all, the men's division is not only reaching new heights. It also has newfound depth.

Evgeny Plushenko

He is "The Natural."

Evgeny Plushenko landed his first triple jump when he was seven years old – and had all six triples mastered by the time he was 13. He also would become the first man to do the aching Biellmann spin, and the first to do a quad-triple-triple combination, the highlight of his 2002–03 season, when he also won his second World Championship.

So there is no reason to doubt his chances of achieving his next goal. "My dream is to do all jumps as quad jumps, even the Axel," Plushenko says. "Every skater wants to do something better, to improve on himself."

Plushenko's been doing that since he was four years old in the southern Russian industrial city of Volgograd. From the first stroke on the ice he was a rarity: a male skater with flexibility, unlimited athletic potential and an innate sense of showmanship. "The Natural." It was just a matter of time, and coaching, until he conquered the world.

As a very young child Plushenko suffered from nose bleeds, and his worried mother, Tatiana, took him to the skating arena, where she had friends, in the hope that his health would improve. "She said I could skate for fun, not for gold medals," he recalls. "Then I won my first competition when I was seven and she said, 'Wow! Maybe now you can skate for medals!'"

She also said that he could do the back-breaking Biellmann spin he had admired a young female skater performing, but only if he practiced it every day, which she made sure he did. He eventually became the first man to do one in competition, and it is now his signature move.

Although Plushenko has been coached by the colorful Alexei Mishin since 1994, his first serious coach was a weightlifter, which explains the incredible power in his jumps. But when he was 11, and the old Soviet Union was in shambles, the arena in Volgograd was turned into a car dealership. He and his mother left his father and sister at home and traveled north to Mishin's famous St. Petersburg school, where Olympic champion Alexei Urmanov and Plushenko's future rival, Alexei Yagudin, were already training.

In a description that would become famous in the skating world, Mishin recalled Plushenko's arrival in St. Petersburg: "He looked like a cheap chicken, very green and very blue and no fat ... very ecological."

Worlds | Vancouver | March 2001

Born: November 3, 1982, Solnechi, Russia

Hometown: St. Petersburg

Training Site: St. Petersburg

Coach: Alexei Mishin

Choreographers: Kiril Smirnov, Valeri Mikhaelovski

RESULTS

2000: 4th Worlds
1st Grand Prix Final
1st Europeans
1st Sparkassen Cup
1st Russian Nationals
1st Cup of Russia
1st NHK

2001: 1st Worlds
1st Grand Prix Final
1st Europeans
1st Russian Nationals
1st Cup of Russia
1st Goodwill Games

2002: 2nd Olympics
1st Grand Prix Final
1st Bofrost Cup
1st Russian Nationals
1st Cup of Russia

2003: 1st Worlds
1st Europeans
1st Grand Prix Final

• Evgeny's mother and father have never seen him in competition, except on television. "It's a tradition," he says.

• Evgeny has more than 40 6.0s in his career.

Worlds | Vancouver | March 2001

Worlds | Vancouver | March 2001

And very poor. Plushenko and his mother shared a small apartment with another family, and Mishin had to pay most of the rent. His family's financial problems provided motivation for Plushenko to train hard every day. He wanted to skate well enough to win prize money to help his family buy an apartment, a dream he eventually realized. His mother and father now live in a large apartment with his two dogs, an American bulldog and an Indian bulldog.

When Plushenko was 14 he landed his first quad, and only 10 days later he had his first quad-triple combination. At the same time, he was developing the intricate spins that only a skater of his flexibility could master. "He can do the Biellmann in both directions," Mishin says. "I didn't do anything for that flexibility. He had it when he came to me because his mother pushed and pulled him to get it."

Quips Plushenko, "Thank you, Mummy."

In 1997, just three years after arriving in St. Petersburg, Plushenko won the world junior title. Later that year, he made his Grand Prix debut, finishing second to Todd Eldredge at Skate America. He was European silver medalist a few months later, but was left off the Russian Olympic team in favor of Yagudin and eventual gold medalist Ilia Kulik. He was back on the team for Worlds a month after the Olympics and made a stunning debut. He had a chance to win but fell three times as

Worlds | Washington | March 2003

he began to ad lib his freeskate program under pressure. Still, he won a bronze medal, a spectacular achievement for a 15-year-old in his first Worlds.

The next year he moved up to second, and at 2000 Worlds Plushenko seemed poised to become the youngest men's champion in history. He'd had a superb season, winning every event he entered, including Europeans. But he was still only 17. He lost his poise in the freeskate, finishing a disappointing fourth.

"I was thinking about medals," he said the next season. "So now, I just skate. I don't think about medals. I think just about jumps."

He got bigger and stronger over the summer – "I grew up" – and ripped through the 2000–01 season winning all but one of his events. This time there was no stopping him at Worlds. He used a different freeskate program for the qualifying rounds and final, the first person ever to do so, and led the competition from wire to wire. No one was even close. The only reason he didn't earn a slew of 6.0s for his freeskate is that there were a couple of top skaters yet to perform.

Plushenko was expected to go head to head with Yagudin for the 2002 Olympic gold, but his rare fall in the short program took him out of that chase. He rallied to win the silver medal.

In 2002–03 Plushenko landed the quad-triple-triple at both the Cup of Russia and Europeans, then despite a very sore left knee, he won his second World Championship. "Naturally."

Worlds | Washington | March 2003

Champions on Ice | Detroit | May 2003

Alexei Yagudin

Alexei Yagudin has nothing left to prove in figure skating, but he's going to prove it anyway. The personable native of St. Petersburg, Russia, says that he will likely stay eligible for the 2006 Olympics, when he could become the first male skater to win two straight Games since Dick Button's second victory in 1952.

Except for a couple of pro-ams in the fall, Yagudin took the 2002–03 season off from competitive skating because of a very painful hip injury that at first threatened to end his entire career. But with rest, therapy and physical rehabilitation, he was able to recover enough to spend the year touring and discovering that, at 23, he was too young to turn professional. "It's hard to be part of these competitions for so many years and then to have it all stop," he explained. "It's really hard on me just to watch."

Like Elvis Stojko before him, he seems to save his best for when it really matters and for when he has to overcome injuries. Yagudin owned the 2002 Olympics, winning the qualifying round, short program and freeskate to dominate the event from beginning to end. He also won his fourth world title a few weeks later in Nagano, Japan, solidifying his reputation as one of the top three or four male skaters of the modern era.

From 1998 to 2000, the expressive Yagudin won three straight world titles, but the one he lost might have been his greatest victory. Just before 2001 Worlds in Vancouver, Yagudin injured his foot while running near his home in Connecticut. By the day before the qualifying round, his 21st birthday, the pain was so severe that he considered withdrawing. But he decided to compete and stumbled through the qualifying round, finishing a disastrous fifth. Doctors advised him to take the rest of the championships off. But he refused, took some injections,

- Alexei has won four world titles, but never the Russian Championships. He has finished second four times.

- "It's still important to win," Alexei says, "but it's not just a competition, it's an event. Like a huge holiday for me."

🔵 Worlds | Vancouver | March 2001

🔵 Olympics | Salt Lake City | February 2002

Born: March 18, 1980, St. Petersburg, Russia

Hometown: St. Petersburg

Training Site: Newington, Connecticut

Coach: Nikolai Morozov

Choreographer: Vladimir Ullanov

RESULTS

2000: 1st Worlds
2nd Europeans
1st Skate Canada
1st Lalique Trophy
2nd Skate America
1st Japan Open

2001: 2nd Worlds
2nd Europeans
2nd Grand Prix Final
1st Japan Open
1st Lalique Trophy
1st Skate Canada

2002: 1st Olympics
1st Worlds
1st Europeans
1st Grand Prix Final

Worlds | Vancouver | March 2001

Worlds | Vancouver | March 2001

Olympics | Salt Lake City | February 2002

and landed quad-triples in both the short program and the freeskate. He won the silver medal, and he completely won over the few remaining fans who doubted his heart. "I wanted to prove that I'm a fighter and a good skater," Yagudin would later say. He didn't have much to prove.

In 1998, just two weeks after his 18th birthday, Yagudin became the second-youngest men's gold medalist in the 102-year history of the World Championships. (Canada's Don McPherson was a week younger when he won in 1963.) He is the only man to win three straight titles without support of the compulsory figures, which were abolished in 1990. And 2001 wasn't the first time he'd shown his warrior side. At the 1998 Olympics, he finished fifth despite skating with flu and a high fever. Because of political in-fighting, he was left off the Russian team for the 1998 Worlds, but was reinstated two weeks before the event. Then, a couple of days before skating, he came down with food poisoning, and still won his first title. In 2000, he crashed into the boards during practice and broke a metacarpal bone 12 days before the European Championships. He arrived with his hand in a cast, but won the short program and finished second overall. A month later, just after his 20th birthday, he won his third straight world title. This is a true athlete.

The international skating community first took notice of Yagudin when, as a high-spirited 14-year-old, he finished fourth at the 1994 Junior Worlds. He was training in St. Petersburg, Russia, with Plushenko and '94 Olympic champion Alexei Urmanov under coach Alexei Mishin.

When Yagudin was born, Russia was still under the Soviet Union's communist system and St. Petersburg was known as Leningrad. Under that regime, skating lessons were provided free, and when Yagudin was four-and-a-half his mother, Zoya, decided to register him, "just to keep me busy." His parents divorced when Alexei was 10, and his father, Konstantin, left for Germany. He hasn't talked much to his father since, a separation that bothers him, "but my mother has been both mother and father to me. She did a lot for me."

Zoya, Alexei and his grandmother Maria lived in a small apartment, which they had to share with another family (a mother and her son) whom they didn't know. "Four rooms. Same bathroom, same kitchen, for both families. My family was poor. It was a really tough time for me. I was just skating, skating, skating and I was like, 'Wow!' First, I was buying a lot of clothes and other stuff for my family. When I was able to buy a flat for my family, I did right away. I'm really glad that you can make

Olympics | Salt Lake City | February 2002

Olympics | Salt Lake City | February 2002

money in skating now, not just to help me, but also to help my family. Because without them I would be no one."

Yagudin left Mishin, and St. Petersburg, after he won his first World Championship to train with skating's grande dame, Tatiana Tarasova, who had just moved to the United States. He felt Mishin was too much of a disciplinarian and was favoring his younger star, Plushenko. That started a long-running public rivalry between the two former clubmates, but Yagudin says, "We can talk. I think we can describe it like Kwan and Lipinski."

Tarasova added a soft, artistic touch to Yagudin's powerful technique arsenal, and by the time he had won his second world title in 1999, he had developed into skating's coveted "complete package." Though four times world champion, paradoxically he has never won his national title, which remains a goal. And it seems that by concentrating on the smaller goals, he gets the bigger ones.

"Before I was thinking just about titles and not about people. I was just going to win," he explains. "Now, every-thing has changed. It's still important to win, but it's not just a competition, it's an event. Like a huge holiday for me.

"But I really wanted the Olympics. That is the win which matters most."

When not touring, Yagudin spends most of his year in Newington, Connecticut, where he plays tennis every day after practice in the off-season. His mother comes to visit for several months each year. Otherwise, he shares his apartment with his cocker spaniel, Lawrie, named after Lawrence of Arabia, one of his most memorable freeskate programs.

Because he's so fond of North American fans, he may eventually take out an American or Canadian passport, "but I will always be Russian in my soul." Still, he feels he doesn't get enough respect in his homeland, and isn't afraid to say so. That outspokenness, combined with his sense of humor and diverse array of skating skills, has won over the North American media.

And his ability to deliver and willingness to fight through pain have won over everybody else.

Timothy Goebel

When people say that Tim Goebel has jumped onto the world podium, that's exactly what they mean.

There is no metaphor here. Goebel himself knows that it is his jumps, his quadruples in particular, which have accelerated him through the ranks. As he is rapidly developing his artistic components to match his profound jumping gifts, Goebel still owns the quad Salchow. "It's my trademark, and really got me noted in the skating world," he acknowledges. He was the first skater to do a quadruple Salchow, the first to do it in combination, the first American to do a quad of any kind and the first skater to include three quads in the same program. He accomplished the last feat in winning a silver medal at Skate America at Colorado Springs in 1999.

"I think that was really my breakthrough into the upper crust of the skating world," Goebel says. "It was the first time I'd won a medal at an international event of such high caliber."

It would not be his last. Goebel won a bronze later that season at the Grand Prix Final. And he narrowly missed the podium at 2001 Worlds, finishing fourth, seven spots better than the previous year's result.

Goebel finally broke into the big time medals in 2001–02 when he won a bronze before an adoring American crowd at the Salt Lake City Olympics. It was the first Olympic medal for U.S. men since 1992, and many experts felt Goebel could have been awarded the silver with his strong performance. A month later, he did win silver at the 2002 Worlds. When he won silver again in 2003 – outperforming champion Evgeny Plushenko technically – he had arrived for good.

Goebel started skating at the age of four in a Chicago suburb and began serious training when he was 10, moving to Lakewood, Illinois, to work with coaches Glyn Watts and Carol Heiss-Jenkins. By 1994 he was U.S. novice

Born: September 10, 1980, Evanston, Illinois

Hometown: Rolling Meadows, Illinois

Training Site: El Segundo, California

Coach: Frank Carroll

Choreographer: Lori Nichol

RESULTS

2000: 11th Worlds
3rd Grand Prix Final
2nd Sparkassen Cup
1st Skate America

2001: 4th Worlds
5th Grand Prix Final
1st Skate America
2nd Sparkassen Cup

2002: 3rd Olympics
2nd Worlds

2003: 2nd Worlds

Worlds | Vancouver | March 2001

- Tim is the first skater to do a total of five quadruples at one World Championship (2001).

- Tim won his first U.S. title in 2001.

champion. Eventually he completed the triple crown by winning the National Junior (1996) and Senior (2001) Championships. At the age of 15, he became the youngest

Worlds | Washington | March 2003

Worlds | Washington | March 2003

U.S. man to land a triple-triple combination, and at the 1997 trials for the Junior Worlds, he became the first American to land three triple jumps in succession.

But it was in March 1998 at the Junior Grand Prix Final that Goebel really grabbed the spotlight. Fourth after the short program, he landed the world's first quadruple Salchow in the freeskate to claim his first international victory.

"My first reaction was relief because I needed it to win," he said. "But I was also proud to be the first American to land a quad. I'd worked on it for about three years."

With his consistency at landing quad jumps, Goebel had worked his way into the consciousness of the judges. But, like many skaters who are pioneers in technical elements, his performances were often one-dimensional. He was so focused on jumps that his skating sometimes seemed almost wooden.

Goebel was aware of this problem, and he worked dili-

gently on his presentation skills. "It's a developmental process," he once said. "You don't just become artistic. I'm a little bit ahead in the jumping, and I always want to keep that edge on everybody. But I want to improve my artistry so that it's even stronger than my technical." That's a tall order, given his technical strengths. But just before 2000 Worlds, feeling he wasn't making enough progress, Goebel left Heiss-Jenkins after a collaboration of nearly a decade. He eventually moved to El Segundo, California, to train under the legendary Frank Carroll, who had been Michelle Kwan's coach. Lori Nichol was also enlisted as his choreographer.

"There's a comfort and communication level that I've not had before," Goebel said of his coaching and choreography team after he won a second successive world silver medal in 2003. "The first year together we were just trying to get comfortable with each other, and the second year there was so much going on – with the Olympics – that there wasn't time for much but training and competing.

But we just clicked this year, and ultimately that makes a big difference."

In his second full year with Carroll and Nichol, Goebel was third at the Olympics and took his first Worlds medal, a silver. In 2002–03, he had to skip the entire Grand Prix season when he developed overuse syndrome in his hip. He struggled through Nationals, where he finished second, but found his rhythm in time for Worlds. His upgraded artistic ability was evident in his "Romeo and Juliet" short program and his "American in Paris" freeskate.

Even though he'd missed most of the season because of his hip, and had severe stomach flu the day of the short program, Goebel won his second successive silver medal at Worlds. His program was technically superior to Evgeny Plushenko's, but he still was behind the world champion artistically. "A lot of my peers had a whole season to work out the kinks in their programs," he said, not at all disappointed in his silver medal. "I think not doing the Grand Prix series was to my detriment. But it was a great comeback from being hurt." The hip injury put on hold Goebel's plans to insert four quads into his freeskate, but he says that's an objective for future seasons, probably beginning in 2003–04.

He'll be right back at jumping into the history books.

Worlds | Washington | March 2003

Champions on Ice | Detroit | May 2003

Takeshi Honda

It's fortunate for Japanese figure skating that the little things – toe picks, for instance – don't discourage Takeshi Honda.

"The first day I figure skated, I caught the toe pick, fell forward and went right onto the ice," the effervescent Honda recalls with a laugh.

When he made that rookie face-plant, Honda was nine years old, and trying to make some sense out of those unfamiliar boots and blades. For two years, he'd been a short-track speed skater like his brother.

Born: March 23, 1981, Koriyama, Japan

Hometown: Koriyama

Training Site: Barrie, Ontario

Coach: Doug Leigh

Choreographers: Kurt Browning, Nikolai Morozov

RESULTS

2000: 10th Worlds
5th Four Continents

2001: 5th Worlds
2nd Four Continents

2002: 4th Olympics
3rd Worlds
2nd Four Continents
1st Skate Canada
3rd Lalique Trophy
2nd NHK

2003: 3rd Worlds
1st Four Continents

Worlds | Vancouver | March 2001

Four Continents | Salt Lake City | February 2001

- Canadian figure skating fans have developed an allegiance to Takeshi. They've adopted him as one of their own.

- Takeshi learned English by watching hundreds of movies on video.

By the time he was 14, Honda had become the youngest-ever Japanese champion, and at 15 he was landing quadruple toe loops in practice. Between 1996 and 2003, he failed to win the National Senior Championship only three times, each when he was forced to withdraw with injury.

Worlds | Washington | March 2003

Worlds | Vancouver | March 2001

And in front of adoring countrymen at the 2002 World Championships in Nagano, Honda won a bronze medal, to become the first Japanese man in 25 years to step onto the podium at Worlds. He had come a long way, figuratively and literally, from his last major appearance in Nagano, when he finished 15th at the 1998 Olympics. To solidify his standing among the world's elite, Honda landed two quadruple jumps in the freeskate at 2003 Worlds and won the bronze medal again.

Honda had been on the scene for so long that it was easy to forget he turned 21 only a few days before winning his first world medal. He has become a more artistic, audience-friendly skater. And he's more consistent with his performances – "just getting the miles on," says his coach, Doug Leigh – and has gained confidence with his presentation skills. "I used to be really good in practice, but when I'd go on the ice for competition I'd lose everything," he recalls. "This time, Nagano was great. Different pressures this time. It was, 'Now I have a chance to get a medal,' not, 'Oh, it's the Olympics – I hope I don't disappoint my countrymen.'"

"I just want to be a world medalist," Honda adds. "It's not that I wanted to be the second Japanese skater to win a medal. My goal is to be world champion. I have to think this way: If I can do my best skate, I can be the champion." With that lofty aim in mind, Honda has been elevating the other components of his repertoire. "His mind caught up with his ability," is how Leigh explains it. "He understands how it goes together. He knows the adjustments he has to make." And, like Leigh students Brian Orser and Elvis Stojko before him, Honda has found the artistic niche to complement his physical assets.

Honda added Nikolai Morozov to help build his 2002–03 programs, and his rapid and entertaining footwork sequences bear the stamp of two years of being choreographed by his childhood idol Kurt Browning. He first met Browning at 1996 Worlds in Edmonton, but the two didn't have a conversation because Honda couldn't speak a word of English. He decided to fix that situation by leaving his insular surroundings in Japan. In late 1997 Honda, then ranked 10th in the world at the age of 16, moved to

Simsbury, Connecticut, to work with Victor Petrenko's coach, Galina Zmievskaya. A few months later he returned to Japan for the '98 Games and, nerve-wracked and under enormous pressure to perform well at home, finished a disappointing 15th. "At that point I was thinking that maybe I would stop skating," he recalls. "But I decided I had just changed everything in my life and wanted to continue. I just said, 'Four more years I will try this.'"

A month after the Olympics he landed his first quad at a World Championship, and by November he had moved from Connecticut to Leigh's Mariposa Skating Club in Ontario. The Japanese skating federation had approached Leigh about working with their medal hope. Stojko was at Mariposa in those days, and Honda absorbed some of the two-time Olympic silver medalist's grit. In 1999, he was the very first winner of the Four Continents Championships, finishing first in the short program and holding off Stojko in the freeskate, having just recovered from an ankle injury.

Honda also turned in an impressive sixth-place finish at Worlds. He had an inconsistent 1999–2000 season and finished 10th at Worlds after missing his combination jump in the short program. But things really began falling into place for him after that. At the Salt Lake City Olympics, he was second with a brilliant short program and was fourth in the freeskate, to finish just off the podium in fourth place, a huge improvement from the 1998 Games. And a month later he won his first medal at Worlds.

In the fall of 2002, Honda won his first Grand Prix event at, appropriately, Skate Canada. For several years Canadian audiences have adopted him as one of their own. They recognize how hard he has worked, not only at skating, but also at adapting to a new language and culture. Skating fans in both his native country and his adopted one think he's got a chance to become the first Japanese man to win a world title.

But instead of being burdened by those hopes, as he once was, he now has the confidence to embrace them. "I got the bronze medal, and it changed my mental thing a lot," Honda explains. "You have to feel, 'I'm a medalist. No one can beat me.' It hasn't changed who I am, but it gives me pride. So I now have to skate my best all the time."

Worlds | Washington | March 2003

Michael Weiss

It seems inevitable that Michael Weiss would become a world-class athlete.

His sister Geremi was silver medalist at the 1990 U.S. Junior Nationals; his other sister, Genna, was world junior diving champion. His mother, Margie, was a collegiate gymnastics champion and is a fitness instructor. And his father, Greg, competed at the 1964 Olympics in Japan as a gymnast. So when Weiss qualified for the 1998 Winter Olympics in Japan, he felt like he'd upheld family tradition. "It's kind of like the circle of life coming back around," he said at the time.

Weiss is an athletic, mature, all-round skater who brings an aggressive, "masculine" style to the sport. And he is a determined athlete. Even after he reached skating's upper ranks, he kept trying the quadruple Lutz, which no one has ever landed.

Weiss was a regional diving champion and began skating at the relatively late age of nine, and he had the same coach, Audrey Weisiger, from then until he switched to Don Laws in October 2002. At 17 he was world junior champ. Weiss won his first of three national senior titles in 1999, with an eight-triple performance, and a month later

Four Continents | Salt Lake City
February 2001

Born:	August 2, 1976, Washington, D.C.
Hometown: McLean, Virginia
Training Site: McLean
Coach: Don Laws
Choreographer: Lisa Thornton-Weiss

RESULTS

2000:	3rd Worlds
	7th Cup of Russia
	1st U.S. Nationals
2001:	3rd Four Continents
	4th U.S. Nationals
	4th Skate America
	8th Sparkassen Cup
2002:	7th Olympics
	6th Worlds
	1st Lalique Trophy
	4th Bofrost Cup
	5th Skate America
2003:	5th Worlds

• In 2003, to help him find competitive consistency and calmness, Michael worked with a hypnotherapist.

landed his first clean quad at Worlds – and won a bronze medal. He took bronze again the next spring.

It's a testament to the U.S. skating depth that, in 2001, a sub-par Weiss could not make the American team for Worlds despite being two-time defending national champion and twice a Worlds bronze medalist.

The setback would only motivate Weiss, who is among the most confident skaters in the United States and who also has a strong support system at home in his wife (Lisa, who is also his choreographer) and two small children. Weiss fought back to make the Olympic and world teams in 2002, although his seventh- and sixth-place finishes were a disappointment. He returned in 2003 to win his first U.S. title in three years and led his qualifying round at Worlds in Washington. But his hopes of winning the world title in his hometown were dashed when he fell on a routine triple Lutz in the short program, leading to a fifth-place finish.

Worlds | Nice | March 2000

◀ Worlds | Washington | March 2003

Chengjiang Li

When he was five years old and living in the northern Chinese city of Changchun, Chengjiang Li saw a seven-year-old girl gracefully stroking her way across the ice surface at a nearby outdoor rink.

At that moment Li decided that figure skating was such a beautiful sport, he wanted to be part of it. The seven-year-old, from the neighboring city of Jilin, was Lu Chen, and 11 years later she became the first Chinese skater to win a World Championship. The boy she inspired became the first Chinese man to win an International Skating Union championship when he captured the 2001 Four Continents title in Salt Lake City.

Li's parents were both skaters, and they eventually became coaches in the figure skating boom that followed Chen's rise to international prominence. But Li is part of a boom of his own. Chinese men have been making a huge impact on the figure skating world, and domestic competition is so fierce that Zhengxin Guo, the first skater to land two quads in a freeskate, did not make the 2001 world team.

Li first gained international notice at the 1998 World Junior Championships in Saint John, New Brunswick. Although he finished seventh, Li became just the second man in history, behind Elvis Stojko, to land quadruple and triple jumps in combination.

At those Junior Worlds, Li displayed little showmanship, laboring with a dour sense of purpose. But American

Born:	April 28, 1979, Changchun, China
Hometown:	Changchun
Training Site:	Beijing
Coach:	Haijun Gao
Choreographers:	Lea Ann Miller, Liu Wei

RESULTS

2001: 7th Worlds
1st Four Continents
3rd Sparkassen Cup
7th Skate America

2002: 9th Olympics
5th Worlds
3rd Bofrost Cup
2nd Cup of Russia
3rd NHK

2003: 4th Worlds
5th Grand Prix Final
3rd Four Continents

choreographer Lea Ann Miller went to work, and within a couple of years Li's natural sense of music had become evident.

And so had his work ethic. At Skate Canada in 1999, Alexei Yagudin was at an early morning practice and marveled at Li landing quad after quad.

"I was just doing spins and a couple of steps," Yagudin said. "I was like, 'Oh my gosh, what's going on with the Chinese guys?' I think he and Timothy (Goebel) will be the skaters of the future."

That future has not fully arrived for Li, but it's getting closer. The four-time national champion has moved from seventh to fifth to fourth at Worlds. And he's given Chinese men's skating its first long-term role model.

- With his seventh-place finish at 2001 Worlds and a sixth by Yunfei Li, Chengjiang helped China qualify three men for the Olympics in 2002.

Worlds | Vancouver | March 2001

 Worlds | Washington | March 2003

Worlds | Vancouver | March 2001

Emanuel Sandhu

Sometimes, success doesn't come until you're mature enough to accept it.

For years, everyone had expected Emanuel Sandhu to establish himself as one of the world's elite skaters. He did exactly that at the 2001 Worlds, finishing ninth overall, including a spectacular fifth-place freeskate. He went one better in 2003, finishing eighth. "It was about growing up," Sandhu said.

There is no tougher place to grow up than on the public stage, which is where Sandhu suddenly found himself after winning a silver medal at the 1998 Nationals. It was his first year in Seniors, and the sensational result was completely unexpected. The Canadian Olympic Association ruled that although Sandhu was the country's second-best men's skater he could not attend the Nagano Olympics because he hadn't performed in enough senior internationals. That decision caused a national uproar and threw the spotlight of controversy on an emotional teenager when he should have been quietly preparing for the Worlds.

Sandhu grew up in Richmond Hill, outside of Toronto. At nine, he was accepted to study at the National Ballet School of Canada. A few months earlier, he had started figure skating, wearing second-hand hockey skates.

Joanne McLeod, who would become his coach, noticed him "skating like a dancer and attempting a two-foot spin, with his ankles inverting in his oversized skates." But she recognized the enormous potential in this lithe spinner. He was supple, graceful and athletic. He had an impeccable ear for music, and he loved to jump.

While Sandhu's results have been wildly inconsistent, he is blessed with immense athletic talent as well as classic artistic sense. In practices he has landed quadruple jumps in combination with three triples.

McLeod thinks 2002–03 was a "transition year" to a more mature training approach for the two-time

Born: November 18, 1980, Toronto, Ontario

Hometown: Vancouver, B.C.

Training Site: Vancouver

Coach: Joanne McLeod

Choreographer: Joanne McLeod

RESULTS

1999: 18th Worlds
10th Four Continents
8th Sparkassen Cup
2nd Canadian Nationals

2000: 13th Four Continents
4th Skate America
6th Sparkassen Cup
2nd Canadian Nationals

2001: 9th Worlds
7th Four Continents
1st Canadian Nationals
5th Skate Canada
9th Lalique Trophy

2002: 2nd Skate Canada
6th Skate America

2003: 8th Worlds
5th Four Continents

Canadians | Saskatoon | January 2003

• Emanuel's balletic style and artistic temperament lead to frequent comparisons with legendary creative forces Toller Cranston and John Curry.

Canadian Champion.

"The torch has finally passed to me," Sandhu said at 2003 Worlds." It's a great feeling."

Ilia Klimkin

When Ilia Klimkin made his debut at the World Championships in 2003, casual skating fans thought his name sounded slightly familiar. But those inside the sport had been expecting him to make it to Worlds much sooner. The Moscow native is a skater blessed with boyish charm and almost unnatural agility, but burdened by inconsistency and the misfortune of growing up in Russia during that country's greatest era of men skaters. So it wasn't until he was 22 years old that Klimkin was finally able to qualify for the World Championships and finish a respectable 10th.

Klimkin owns a critical piece of figure skating history. He pushed the quadruple revolution significantly forward in 1999, when he became the first skater to execute two different quads in the same program. He landed both the quad toe loop and the quad Salchow at the 1999 Nebelhorn Trophy in Oberstdorf, a German mountain town rich with skating history. That was his first foray into senior international competition, but it also came during the most tumultuous season of his life. His father had died a couple of years earlier and Ilia's coach, Igor Rusakov, was in Paris taking treatment for leukemia.

Klimkin has often been called the most innovative newcomer to figure skating over the past decade. Some of his body contortions defy description. He is so flexible that in his spread eagle, he bends backward at the knees so that his back is almost parallel to the ice and manages to hold that position as he glides around the surface. His unique arsenal of elements includes spins in both directions, a cantilever and a camel spin from which he launches into a triple Salchow.

Klimkin's struggle to find an even competitive keel is reflected in his three appearances at World Juniors. In between fourth-place finishes in 1998 and 2000, he won the title in 1999. In 2001–02, he was 11th at the Goodwill Games but also won the Finlandia Trophy and reached the podium at Russian Nationals. "I'll try to make my fans happier more often by skating better," he vowed at the time. He kept his promise. The next season he won NHK, finished second at the Grand Prix Final and finally made it to his first Worlds.

- Ilia had three serious operations during the summer of 2002 to mend broken blood vessels in his right leg. But he was back on the ice in September – and had his best season.

Born: August 15, 1980, Moscow

Hometown: Moscow

Training Site: Moscow

Coach: Igor Rusakov

Choreographer: Irina Kolganova

RESULTS

2001: 4th Russian Nationals
5th Cup of Russia
1st Top Jump

2002: 6th Europeans
3rd Russian Nationals
7th Lalique Trophy
1st NHK

2003: 10th Worlds
4th Europeans
2nd Grand Prix Final
2nd Russian Nationals

Worlds | Washington | March 2003

- Ilia's grandmother took him to the rink when he was four, but he hated skating and wanted to play soccer instead.

- Ilia's skating role models are Brian Orser, Brian Boitano and Robin Cousins.

Brian Joubert

Brian Joubert wanted to be a hockey player – so maybe that's where he gets his battling spirit. Since he burst onto the world scene in 2002, the young French skater has been known for his high energy, youthful exuberance and unwillingness to quit when odds are stacked against him.

When skating observers say Joubert has come out of nowhere, they partly mean an almost anonymous rink in the town of Poitiers, where he is still taught by his first and only coach, Veronique Guyon. He is the only elite skater at the rink, but refuses to leave the place of his birth. "I want to stay with Veronique," he says forcefully. "If she stays in Poitiers, then I'm going to stay in Poitiers." Since most of the political power in French skating rests in Paris, Joubert took a gamble with his stand, but he's got the goods to back it up.

Until 2002, however, no one really knew Joubert had those goods. In his only appearance at Junior Worlds, he finished 15th. Joubert had gained a little fame when he came second at the 2001 Top Jump competition by landing a quadruple toe/triple toe loop combination, but he finished a discouraging 14th at the French Nationals in 2001. Then came his huge breakthrough. With reliable quads in his arsenal, Joubert was the surprise bronze medal winner at the 2002 European Championships.

He was named to France's Olympic team and finished 14th, but he and China's Min Zhang were the only skaters outside the top 10 to land quads in the freeskate. He moved up only one place at Worlds a month later. But the 2002–03 season firmly established Joubert as a future contender. Working with renowned choreographer Nikolai Morozov, he is honing his gently masculine, charismatic style. He won Skate America, finished third in the Grand Prix Final and then took the silver medal at the European Championships. At the 2003 Worlds in Washington, Joubert got off to a horrible start, falling three times, struggling to ninth place in his qualifying group. But he fought back to finish sixth overall, in just his second Worlds.

He might have come out of nowhere, but he's definitely somewhere now.

Born: September 20, 1984, Poitiers, France

Hometown: Poitiers

Training Site: Poitiers

Coach: Veronique Guyon

Choreographer: Nikolai Morozov

RESULTS

2001: 2nd Top Jump
9th Skate America
14th French Nationals

2002: 14th Olympics
13th Worlds
3rd Europeans
3rd French Nationals
1st Skate America

2003: 6th Worlds
2nd Europeans
3rd Grand Prix Final
1st French Nationals

Worlds | Washington | March 2003

- Brian wanted to play hockey, but his mother signed him up for figure skating lessons.

- He is enrolled in a special sports correspondence school so he can concentrate on his skating while taking his studies.

- Brian has landed three different quadruple jumps (Salchow, flip, toe loop) in practice.

Jeff Buttle

Jeff Buttle may have taken everyone else by surprise, but not himself. So when he enjoyed a breakthrough season in 2001–02, he showed the kind of confidence that is common among athletes at Canada's Mariposa Skating Club. "I was definitely planning on it, but I wasn't sure of just when it was going to happen," laughs Buttle, who was born in Sudbury, Ontario, but trains two hours south in Barrie.

After never finishing higher than sixth, Buttle took his first national senior medal at the 2002 Canadians in Hamilton, Ontario, when he sparkled his way to third place. But he had already served notice that he could be a contender with a solid autumn season. He was second at the second-tier Nebelhorn Trophy attempt, then

Worlds | Washington | March 2003

moved up to the Grand Prix Circuit and shocked the skating world with a silver medal at the prestigious NHK Championship. A few weeks after his bronze at Nationals, he won the Four Continents Championship in his first appearance. Although he wasn't named to Canada's Olympic team, he once again created shock waves when he finished eighth at his debut Worlds.

What was most surprising about Buttle's excellent season was that he had such strong finishes without having mastered a triple Axel in combination with another triple, or a quadruple, jump. But while short on those big tricks, he had a lot of other assets. His electric personality burns through brightly, no matter how well he's doing on the technical elements. In that regard, he's a figure skating rarity, because his artistic side matured more quickly than his mechanical side did.

But Buttle trains with Wendy Phillion, Lee Barkell and Doug Leigh, who all helped turn Mariposa into the quad capital of the world when Elvis Stojko was the star student. So it wasn't shocking that in the course of just one off-season, Buttle was able to get not only a quad, but also a quad combination into his repertoire. He and Barkell decided at the start of the 2002–03 season that Buttle would try the quad-triple combination in the short program at every event, no matter what. Most of the season

Born: September 1, 1982, Smooth Rock Falls, Ontario

Hometown: Sudbury, Ontario

Training Site: Barrie, Ontario

Coaches: Lee Barkell, Wendy Phillion, Doug Leigh

Choreographer: David Wilson

RESULTS

2001: 7th World Juniors
9th Canadian Nationals
2nd NHK
2nd Nebelhorn Trophy
3rd Karl Schafer Memorial

2002: 8th Worlds
1st Four Continents
3rd Canadian Nationals
5th NHK
3rd Sears Open
7th Skate Canada

2003: 15th Worlds
4th Four Continents
2nd Canadian Nationals

• In 2001, Jeff started taking chemical engineering classes at the University of Toronto. He skated in the morning, then drove more than an hour to school.

he fell on the combination, but he still had some solid finishes: third at the Sears Open, fifth at NHK and second at the Canadian Championships.

At the Four Continents in Beijing, Buttle finished fourth, but finally nailed the quadruple toe loop/triple toe loop combination. He was ecstatic. "That was a pretty big thing and I got a little excited and stiff in the knees after that, so my triple Axel and Lutz suffered," Buttle said. At 2003 Worlds in Washington, Buttle got off to a good start with a sixth in his qualifying group and eighth in the short program. But a disastrous 19th in the freeskate left him 15th overall. It was a disappointing end to the season. Still, Buttle had already demonstrated that, with a few more "miles" on his quad to go with his engaging on-ice presence, he can be among the world's elite skaters.

Ryan Jahnke

If good things come to those who wait, and good things come to those who believe in other people, then Ryan Jahnke was long overdue for some good things. The 2002–03 season finally brought them to him. Ten years after he won the U.S novice title, and five years after his first senior competition, the modest athlete finally stepped onto the podium at U.S. Nationals and was named to his first world team.

The official practices for the 2003 World Championships in Washington began on the very day Jahnke turned 25 years old. "I've had an incredible amount of disappointment in my skating career," Jahnke concedes. "But suffering is one of those things that make you stronger. After a failure you can get bitter or you can get stronger." Jahnke chose the latter.

There was little that indicated Jahnke was about to break out of the mold that had seen him place eighth three times and fifth and ninth once each in his previous appearances at Senior Nationals. He was sixth in the 2003 short program, but with others wavering he finished a stunning second in the freeskate to claim the bronze medal in one of the most emotionally gratifying moments of the American skating season.

Jahnke had refused to give up on himself or on his coach, Diana Ronayne. She had been his principal mentor and influence for over a decade in Grosse Point Farms, Michigan, when she accepted the job of skating director at the prestigious Colorado Springs World Arena in 1999. After a promising start for Jahnke – he won the U.S. novice title in 1993, the year before Tim Goebel did – his career had stalled, with no quadruple jump and inconsistencies in other elements. Ronayne's departure provided a perfect opportunity to switch coaches, but Jahnke followed her west.

Born: March 21, 1978, Detroit

Hometown: Grosse Point Farms, Michigan

Training Site: Colorado Springs

Coaches: Diana Ronayne, Hoon Kim

Choreographer: Tom Dickson

RESULTS

2000: 12th Four Continents
5th U.S. Nationals
6th Lalique Trophy
8th Nebelhorn Trophy

2001: 8th U.S. Nationals
9th Nebelhorn Trophy

2002: 8th U.S. Nationals
5th Finlandia Trophy

2003: 3rd Worlds
6th Four Continents
3rd U.S. Nationals

Worlds | Washington | March 2003

- Ryan didn't take figure skating seriously until he was 11. Before that he skated because he wanted to play hockey.

- Ryan, who teaches Sunday School, was voted role model of the year by the Broadmoor Skating Club.

That loyalty paid some unexpected dividends. Jahnke met his future wife, Tashiana, in Colorado Springs, and he was able to work with World Arena coach Hoon Kim on improving his technical shortcomings. Kim got him to relax, and his jumps improved. Jahnke also took up coaching young skaters. After his gratifying bronze medal, Jahnke had a strong start at the World Championships, finishing third in his qualifying group and ninth in the short program. But he landed only one clean triple in the freeskate and finished 13th overall. Still, he felt it had been a watershed season for him: "This is the beginning of what I see as new territory in my career."

Alexander Abt

One of these years, the injury gods will finally smile on Alexander Abt and let him show the world exactly what he can do.

As far back as 1993, Russian journalists were touting Abt as the next great Russian skater, but he's had misfortune after misfortune since then. Abt was named to the Russian team for the 1995 Europeans, but he couldn't skate because of an injured hip. Knee surgery kept him out of the Russian Nationals in 1996, and a second knee operation in late 1998 ruined the rest of that season as well.

But the most debilitating injury came at a rink in Mexico, when the Russian team was on tour during the summer of 1996. The practice ice was "disgusting," Abt says, and he caught a rut, sending him into the boards. His left skate sliced into the quadriceps muscle on his right leg. He spent six months in hospital, undergoing surgery twice.

"The doctors told me I would not walk at all, and there was no talk of a return to sport," Abt recalled. "I relearned to walk, then later, to stand on the skates. Like a child. That year and a half was like remaking the wheel."

He also had to remake all his jumps and didn't have his triple Axel for the next season. But by 1997–98, his remarkable physical comeback was complete. He got a berth to his first Europeans and won a bronze. But by late December, he was back in the hospital for another knee surgery.

In April 1999 Abt married former ice dancer Elena Pavlova, and their son, Makar, was born 11 months later.

"My life will be brighter and better," he said. And it was. In 2000, he made the Grand Prix Final, won his first medal, at Nationals and finished sixth in his debut at Worlds.

But Abt suffered a sinus infection during 2001 Europeans, and required surgery for it in 2002. But that didn't stop him from winning the silver medal at

Born: October 22, 1976, Moscow

Hometown: Montclair, New Jersey

Training Site: Montclair

Coach: Alexander Zhulin

Choreographer: Alexander Zhulin

RESULTS

2000: 6th Worlds
4th Europeans
4th Grand Prix Final
4th Sparkassen Cup
5th Skate America
5th Cup of Russia

2001: 8th Worlds
4th Europeans
3rd Skate America
4th Sparkassen Cup

2002: 5th Olympics
4th Worlds
2nd Europeans
2nd Skate America
2nd Bofrost Cup
3rd Cup of Russia

2003: 4th Grand Prix Final

Olympics | Salt Lake City | February 2002

Europeans and finishing fourth at Worlds. The injury bug bit again in 2003, however, as a leg injury forced him to withdraw from Europeans and Worlds.

"Unfortunately," he said, "I already know what it means to be unlucky. I just try to do the best that I can."

- Alexander's musical sense is renowned. When he's healthy, his skating is "the total package."

Stanick Jeannette

Stanick Jeannette has the potential – but can't always turn it into reality. Jeannette, an entertaining and innovative skater from a Paris suburb, had been viewed as a future celebrity ever since he was 15 and won the French Junior Nationals.

But he has been unable to find consistency from year to year or, often, from event to event. Something always seemed to prevent him from reaching and maintaining his highest performance level. Injuries and misfortune have played a role in this. In 1994, for example, he required surgery to a tendon, and in 1998 his skate blade broke during French Nationals. His former coach, Pierre Trente, once said, "With Stanick you have skating in its purest form – skating with real emotion. But when is he going to get his act together?"

Jeannette got his act together to win his first French Nationals in late 1999 at the age of 22 and finally represented his country at Europeans and Worlds. He had a very strong seventh-place finish at Worlds, after finishing only ninth at Europeans. The next season, he seemed to have arrived for good when he won a bronze medal at Europeans, but then he sagged to 11th at Worlds. And the next year, 2001, he failed to qualify for either competition after he came a disastrous fifth at French Nationals.

Jeannette's role model was the inventive Canadian skater Gary Beacom, a brilliant and unorthodox performer of the 1980s and 1990s. That influence is reflected in Jeannette's body lines, impressive showmanship and creative spins. But like many of the most artistic skaters, Jeannette was often the victim of his own emotions. His new coach, Philippe Pelissier, and his choreographer, Olympic dance champion Gwendal Peizerat, work on helping him control those emotions.

When he regained his place on the French world team with a silver medal at French Nationals in 2003, Jeannette said he needed "to recover the confidence I lacked last season. I had to show I was consistent." He followed his silver at French Nationals with a bronze medal at the 2003

Born: March 6, 1977, Courbevoie, France

Hometown: Cergy, France

Training Site: Paris

Coaches: Philippe Pelissier, Pasquale Camerlengo

Choreographer: Gwendal Peizerat

Skate Canada | Quebec City | October 2002

RESULTS

2001: 11th Worlds
6th Grand Prix Final
3rd Europeans
1st French Nationals
11th Skate Canada

2002: 5th French Nationals
4th Skate Canada
4th Lalique Trophy

2003: 16th Worlds
3rd Europeans
2nd French Nationals

• Stanick's freeskate music in 2002–03 was composed especially for him by Maxim Rodriguez. "Choreography is like language," says Stanick, who speaks it fluently.

Europeans, as he and silver medalist Brian Joubert gave France its first double podium appearance there in 10 years.

THE WOMEN

Michelle Kwan

Sasha Cohen

Fumie Suguri

Sarah Hughes

Irina Slutskaya

Elena Liashenko

Elena Sokolova

Jennifer Robinson

Victoria Volchkova

Yoshie Onda

Jennifer Kirk

Joannie Rochette

Over the last half-decade of the 20th century and the early part of the 21st, there have been two dominant themes and one dominant individual in women's figure skating. The dominant themes are age and the New Cold War between the United States and Russia.

The dominant personality, Michelle Kwan, has been central to both. Kwan's brilliance and consistency have earned her a spot among the all-time greats of her sport, but Kwan has also personified the demographics of her dynamic era. She hit the world scene as a 13-year-old alternate on the U.S. team at the 1994 Olympics – won by Oksana Baiul, then the second-youngest gold medalist in history. In 1998, Kwan finished second to the youngest winner ever, Tara Lipinski, who immediately turned professional, at the age of 15. Kwan was just 17 at the time, the same age Sarah Hughes was four years later when she

surprised Kwan and Irina Slutskaya, not to mention the rest of the world, and won the 2002 Olympics.

Through all those downs and ups – she has won five world titles and a staggering eight straight world medals – Kwan has often joked that she felt "old" trying to fend off waves of young challengers. But as she has remained in eligible ranks and matured, Kwan has also forced women's skating to mature along with her.

It helped that after the premature losses of Baiul and Lipinski to the pros, the International Skating Union came up with new minimum-age requirements for Worlds. There are still strong young challengers, but fewer of them. The youngest competitor at 2003 Worlds was superstar-in-waiting Carolina Kostner, who was 16. Choreography has become far more sophisticated and creative. And because prize money has made eligible ("amateur") skating financially rewarding, more top skaters have resisted the urge to turn professional.

Thus, the same period that produced the ballistic youngsters also featured the oldest women's world champion ever. Maria Butyrskaya was 26 when she won at Helsinki in 1999. She finally left the Olympic-eligible ranks in 2002. Butyrskaya's was the first world title ever won by a Russian woman, but it wouldn't be the last. For decades, Russia (then part of the Soviet Union) did not produce notable women's single skaters. The nation's best females were funneled into either pairs or dance. But by the mid-1990s, Russians had become as important a force in

women's singles as Americans had. Elena Sokolova, who'd been absent from the larger world scene for nearly five years, won the silver medal at 2003 Worlds, constant challenger Viktoria Volchkova was fifth, and the likes of Julia Soldatova and Kristina Oblasova were nipping at their heels back home.

And in 2002, Kwan's longtime friend and rival Irina Slutskaya finally beat her for the world title. They had competed head-to-head since Junior competitions in the early 1990s, with Kwan's elegant combination of artistry and smooth jumps finishing ahead of Slutskaya's fiercely defiant athleticism every time a World Championship was on the line. The Kwan–Slutskaya duel of contrasting styles is a compelling one. "It's so hard because each of us is unique in our own way," says Kwan. "Irina's a really good person and you want her to do well and you want yourself to do well, and there's only one first place."

In the United States, where the women's division is the one that matters most to the general public, there remains a bountiful harvest of contenders. Kwan is backed by Hughes (who has been considering taking time off from

skating to attend college), the dynamic Sasha Cohen, Ann Patrice McDonough, Jennifer Kirk and several other younger skaters. So, it should have come as no surprise that even though the anticipated 1-2-3 sweep by Americans did not occur, five of the top six at 2003 Worlds came from Russia or the United States.

The only exception was Fumie Suguri, the popular 22-year-old from Japan. And her second successive world bronze medal may have been the forerunner to the arrival of the next great national power in women's skating. Suguri is the oldest of a spectacular group of Japanese females who came into the sport idolizing the country's two world champions, triple Axel pioneer Midori Ito (1989 champion) and the "skater's skater," Yuka Sato (1994). In fact, Sato's father is Suguri's coach. Among potential future world champions from Japan are Yoshie Onda, who was fifth in 2002; Shizuka Arawaka, eighth in 2003; world Junior champion Yukino Ota; Yukari Nakano, who helped break the decade-long triple Axel drought in women's skating at 2002 Skate America; and Mika Ando, who landed history's first quadruple jump by a woman at the 2003 Junior Grand Prix Final.

After a long lull in pushing the technical envelope, the women are back at it in full force. Slutskaya, who missed 2003 Worlds because of a family illness, has a triple-triple-double combination; a pubescent Japanese skater has strung together three triples in a row; and Kostner hit two triple-triples in her freeskate at 2003 Europeans. By the 2006 Olympics, it will take at least one triple-triple combination, and perhaps two triple-triples or a triple Axel, as well as mature artistry for a skater to stand atop the podium. And, combined with more competition-hardened fields, that can only be good for women's skating.

Michelle Kwan

As Michelle Kwan finished her exquisite freeskate at the 2003 World Championships, the Washington audience leapt to its feet with a deafening roar. They weren't cheering only for what Kwan had just done: become the first woman to reclaim her World Championship on three separate occasions; move into a tie with legends Dick Button and Carol Heiss as the only Americans with five world titles; extend to eight straight years her string of winning gold or silver at Worlds. They were also cheering for who she is. They were celebrating her composure, her era-defining decade at Worlds, her graceful acceptance of the good and the bad, her dedication to and love for skating, and her incredible resiliency.

Michelle Kwan was right at the top again, just a few months after her second successive Olympic heartbreak. In 1998 she won Olympic silver in a close battle with Tara Lipinski, and four years later she took the bronze medal at the Salt Lake City Games, a marvelous achievement, but two huge spots short of her longtime goal. But instead of retreating, Kwan returned in 2002–03, albeit with a vastly reduced schedule and a new coach (Scott Williams) – and she defeated yet another bunch of young contenders. "I still don't believe it," she beamed. "I have no words. When I look back at 10 years of Worlds, it seems like it didn't happen."

Kwan was already well known in American skating circles by the time she came to the world's attention in 1994 as the most famous Olympic alternate in skating history. She was just 13 when she finished second at U.S. Nationals and was sent to the Lillehammer Olympics as a substitute in case Nancy Kerrigan – injured in the infamous incident involving Tonya Harding – couldn't skate.

The attention from the Kerrigan–Harding circus helped groom Kwan for her starring roles in three of the most memorable duels in women's skating history. In 1996,

Born: July 7, 1980, Torrance, California

Hometown: Torrance

Training Site: Los Angeles

Coach: Scott Williams

RESULTS

2000: 1st Worlds
2nd Grand Prix Final
1st Skate America

2001: 1st Worlds
2nd Grand Prix Final
1st Skate America
3rd Skate Canada

2002: 3rd Olympics
2nd Worlds
2nd Grand Prix Final
1st Skate America

2003: 1st Worlds

Worlds | Washington | March 2003

• Michelle has written several books including *Michelle Kwan: Heart of a Champion* and *The Winning Attitude*.

• *People* magazine has chosen Michelle as one of the "50 Most Beautiful People in the World."

Kwan and Chen Lu of China each received two perfect 6.0s for their artistry, the only time that's ever happened in a women's freeskate at the World Championships. Kwan, just 15, edged the refined defending champion for her first world title. Both women are known for their trademark elegance, gentle landings and flowing interpretation of music. At the 1998 Nagano Winter Games, Kwan skated superbly enough to win any other Olympics. But in a 6–3 judging split, her 15-year-old American rival, Lipinski, became the youngest Olympic champion ever. The gracious manner in which Kwan handled her emotionally devastating defeat inspired the audience at the World Championships in Minneapolis a month later to give her a standing ovation before she skated.

In 2001, there was the classic confrontation of styles between the exquisite Kwan, skating to "Song of the Black Swan," and the athletic Irina Slutskaya, who landed the world's first triple-triple-double combination by a woman. The two good friends had been competing against each other since Junior Worlds in 1994, and Slutskaya seemed to be surpassing Kwan, beating her in two head-to-head skates in the 2000–01 season. But Kwan attacked her program with fervor and her usual dignity and finished to a wild standing ovation – to become the first four-time American world champion since 1960. "When I finished the program and they were all on their feet, I just wanted to put it all in a little bottle and keep it forever," she said.

Kwan and Slutskaya were expected to battle it out for the gold medal again the next year at the Salt Lake City Olympics. Just four months before the Olympics, Kwan parted ways with coach Frank Carroll, whom she'd been with since she was 11. "I love Frank, and he's a great coach, but as I've gotten older I've gotten more independent, and I think for myself," Kwan explained at the time. "And that's the way it should be." Her unprecedented move of coming to the Olympics without a coach raised a lot of eyebrows in the skating world, especially when she finished third behind surprise winner Sarah Hughes and Slutskaya. Kwan was devastated, but once again she handled the crushing disappointment with the class and good sportsmanship that had become synonymous with her and her family.

Danny Kwan and his wife, Estella, came to California from Hong Kong in the early 1970s, and opened a restaurant in Torrance. They had three children, Ron, Karen and Michelle, the youngest. Michelle began skating at the age of five after watching Ron play hockey. Karen also skated, and in 1995 they became the first sisters to compete against each other in Senior Nationals in 36 years. The Kwans are a close family and Michelle never competes without wearing a Chinese good luck charm around her neck. It was given to her by her grandmother. "My grandmother, my grandfather, my parents, they're all hard workers," Michelle

says. "They have taught me so much. I think I'm very fortunate to have such a tight family … very supportive and loving. I think that's made a difference in my skating."

And Kwan has made a huge difference in skating. At 13, she became the youngest U.S. Olympic Festival champion ever, setting the tone for a future of record-breaking performances. The most stunning was at the 1998 Nationals, when she received 15 perfect marks for presentation – seven in the short program and eight in the freeskate. By 1999, she was a 19-year-old freshman living in a dormitory at UCLA, still at the top of the skating world and trying to study on airplanes. At first, it was difficult to strike a balance between school and skating, and she struggled much of the season. But she peaked in time to win the 2000 Worlds after losing to Maria Butyrskaya the previous spring. She had become the first skater to reclaim the world title twice in her career.

Worlds | Washington | March 2003

Worlds | Washington | March 2003

"It just felt very satisfying to come back strong after so many people had said, 'Oh, she's over; oh, she's deteriorating.'" Those people have since learned never to say anything like that about Michelle Kwan again.

Sasha Cohen

She may be small in stature, but she is a huge talent. Alexandra Pauline Cohen – better known as Sasha – is accustomed to making a big impression. She came within a whisker of winning an Olympic medal before she had even appeared at a World Championship. She finished second at the cut-throat U.S. Nationals just a few weeks after her 15th birthday. As she turned 17, she was blithely attempting quadruple Salchows in Senior fall internationals. Throughout it all, she often argued toe-to-toe with one of the gruffest coaches in the business. "She stands up for what she believes in," that coach, John Nicks, once said. "She's a unique person whose talents transcend the technical elements."

Cohen is one of the world's most mesmerizing skaters, with an ideal fusion of power and grace. She still lacks the consistency of the great champions, perhaps a by-product of rising so high so quickly. When many of her current opponents were competing at the 1998 Olympics, Cohen was still a Novice skater, finishing only 6th at Nationals. In 1999, Cohen finished second at Junior Nationals, but the next year she was second to Michelle Kwan in Seniors. She was still too young (15) to qualify for the World Championships.

Growing up in Laguna Niguel, California, Cohen began her athletic career as a gymnast. She won several important meets before opting for figure skating when she was seven years old. With her gymnastic background, Cohen is among the most flexible skaters in the world and rotates easily in her jumps and spins. Many observers felt she would be the first woman to land the elusive quadruple jump, but she put that project on the backburner as she began to chase down a world medal. "I think something I have worked on that maybe some other skaters have neglected is spins," she says of her supple style. "I really work on positioning and speed. In the spirals, too."

Cohen's signature move is a magnificent spiral, in which she glides effortlessly across the ice in complete control, with one leg extended almost straight up in the air above her head. Such fluidity helps her collect high presentation marks, and when her jumps are on she's difficult to defeat. Often, though, she would defeat herself, as she did with faltering freeskates to finish fourth at both the 2002 Olympics and Worlds. That was one of the first things superstar coach Tatiana Tarasova addressed when

Born: October 28, 1984, Westwood, California

Hometown: Avon, Connecticut

Training Site: Simsbury, Connecticut

Coach: Tatiana Tarasova

Choreographer: Tatiana Tarasova

RESULTS

2000: 6th World Juniors
2nd U.S. Nationals

2001: 1st Finlandia
Trophy

2002: 4th Olympics
4th Worlds
2nd U.S. Nationals
1st Skate Canada
1st Lalique Trophy
2nd Cup of Russia

2003: 4th Worlds
1st Grand Prix
Final

Skate Canada | Quebec City
October 2002

- When Sasha decided to leave coach John Nicks for Tatiana Tarasova in 2002, her whole family made the move too, so she would not have to live alone on the east coast.

- During the opening ceremonies of the 2002 Winter Olympics, Sasha brashly handed President Bush her cell phone so he could speak to her mother.

- One of Sasha's long-term goals is to be a fashion designer.

Worlds | Washington | March 2003

Worlds | Washington | March 2003

Cohen switched coaches and arrived at her training center in Simsbury, Connecticut, in the autumn of 2002. "The most important thing I've learned is to skate against myself, and not against everyone else's self," Cohen said of the move from the west coast to the east coast. "I am a better competitor now. Tatiana is very much like me. We're both very emotional people, both a little impatient. We want the best out of me and we want it now."

An independent thinker, Cohen does not pretend that she was happy with finishing fourth at the 2002

Worlds | Washington | March 2003

Worlds | Washington | March 2003

Olympics. She had been third after the short program but, approaching the freeskate tentatively and nervously, she made several mistakes and dropped off the podium. It was still a tremendous achievement for a teenager who'd missed most of the previous competitive season with a back injury, but Cohen regretted that she hadn't been more aggressive. Besides fine-tuning her student's jumps, Tarasova was able to convince Cohen that she had to attack her freeskating program element by element, instead of looking too far ahead. While Cohen's relationship with Nicks was fiery and sometimes combative, she usually listens attentively to everything her new coach has to say, even in Russian. Cohen's mother, Galina, emigrated to the United States from Ukraine, and Sasha says she understands almost everything Tarasova is telling her.

Although Cohen and Tarasova got a late start together on the 2002–03 campaign, it turned into the skater's best season yet. There was still a disappointing letdown in the freeskate at U.S. Nationals, when Cohen dropped back to third place, but she won two Grand Prix events and was second in another. And after trailing Irina Slutskaya through the short program and first freeskate (there are two) at the Grand Prix Final, she unleashed a stirring second freeskate to overcome the Russian star and win her first major international title. That was Slutskaya's only loss at the Grand Prix Final in five years. Cohen finished fourth again at 2003 Worlds, but not because of her former problem of faltering in the freeskate. She was fifth in the short program and moved up by placing third in the freeskate.

"I've improved a lot every year, but I have to be really happy about where I am now," she says. "I'm a smarter skater. I'm really excited to see what it will be like to work with Tatiana for a whole year." Her opponents probably aren't quite as excited about the idea.

Fumie Suguri

At an age when most elite athletes are already competing internationally, Fumie Suguri had not even started skating seriously. "I spent a lot of time with skating just as a hobby," says the two-time world bronze medalist. "I didn't practice enough. I was only skating one hour a day, and just for fun. I didn't start real training, like an athlete, until I was nearly 15 years old." But once she dedicated herself to the sport, Suguri proved to be a natural. It took her only two years to win her first Japanese championship.

It was another four years before she won her next one, however, because her career was affected by injuries, politics within her national federation, and the demands of rigorous schooling. In the Suguri family, the skating of Fumie and her younger sister, Chika, always took a back seat to a good education. Suguri went to a private high school in Yokohama, where expectations were high and homework was heavy, so she had time for only limited training.

But when she finished 11th at Junior Nationals in 1995, Suguri "was disappointed in myself," and realized that she had to spend more time on the ice if she wanted better results. She increased her training time to three hours each day, began working off-ice with weights, somehow found the time to prepare for the difficult Japanese university entrance exams, and within a year was able to land all five triple jumps. She also hired Canada's Lori Nichol, Michelle Kwan's choreographer, and the two have worked together ever since. "Michelle was my favorite skater, and I loved her programs," Suguri said. "That's why I asked Lori to do my programs. I was lucky she had the time to do them for me."

Although Suguri showed plenty of promise, her career sputtered after her first national title in 1997. For three straight seasons she was bothered by a variety of injuries and was rarely in peak physical form. She finished 18th at her first Worlds in 1997, then missed both the 1998 Olympics and Worlds because she finished second at Nationals and Japan had only one berth. Jumping sensation Shizuka Arakawa, who had made the leap directly from Juniors, won her only Senior national title that year and was named Japan's representative to the Nagano Olympics. "I went to Nagano just to watch," Suguri recalls. "I didn't really feel good, but it was a good experience to learn just how disappointed I was, and not let that happen again."

Born: December 31, 1980, Chiba, Japan

Hometown: Toyko

Training site: Kanagawa

Coaches: Nobuo Sato, Kumiko Sato

Choreographer: Lori Nichol

RESULTS

2001: 7th Worlds
1st Four Continents
3rd Skate Canada
7th NHK
3rd Goodwill Games

2002: 5th Olympics
3rd Worlds
2nd Skate Canada
2nd Bofrost Cup
4th NHK

2003: 3rd Worlds
1st Four Continents
6th Grand Prix Final

- Fumie's father is an airline pilot and moved the family to Alaska for two years when she was three. Her mother took her to the skating rink in Yokohama at age six because, Fumie says, "she wanted my body to remember all the good outdoor things we did in Alaska."

Four Continents | Salt Lake City | February 2001

She had left her original coach, Nobuko Fukui, for Shinji Someya, who was renowned for teaching the technical elements. But eventually they too parted company, so Suguri went to the 1999 Worlds without a coach and finished a humbling 20th. "It was not the right decision," she admits. Before the 1999–2000 season, Suguri was

Worlds | Washington | March 2003

Four Continents | Salt Lake City | February 2001

thinking about a move to North America. But she was accepted into a local university, and she wanted to study social science. So, in what became a career-enhancing move, she switched to another coach at her home rink – highly regarded Nobuo Sato, the father and coach of 1994 world champion Yuka Sato. Yuka's mother is also part of Suguri's coaching team. Suguri has already been favorably compared with her coaches' daughter.

Yuka Sato presented a graceful, well-rounded contrast to Midori Ito's spectacular athleticism. So, too, Fumie Suguri is a beacon of elegance amidst a new generation of Japanese leapers. During the 2003 Worlds, television commentator and former Olympic dance medalist Tracy Wilson called Suguri "the skater's skater" because of her use of edges and footwork. That's a label which has often been applied to Sato. "I want to show my flow, my edges and also my spins," said Suguri, who has the perfect choreographing ally in Nichol.

In her first year with the Satos, Suguri was bothered by injuries to both ankles and finished only third at Japanese Nationals. In a haunting reprise of 1998, Japan had only one representative for 2000 Worlds, and the federation selected another jumper just out of Juniors, Yoshie Onda. "That kind of hurt," recalls Suguri, who had beaten Onda at both Nationals and the Four Continents.

But things were about to change drastically. The 2000–01 season demonstrated what a healthy Suguri can do. She finished third at Skate Canada, her first international medal in two years, then won the Four Continents. "I was really surprised. I was looking for the podium, but not first," she says. "Also," she adds modestly, "I was a bit lucky because other good skaters had trouble with the short program."

She showed that it wasn't all luck when she delivered a stunning, but undermarked, short program at 2001 Worlds. She finished seventh overall, a mercurial rise of

Skate Canada | Quebec City | October 2002

Four Continents | Salt Lake City | February 2001

13 places over her previous appearance. But she wasn't satisfied. "It was a good season, but my coach and I were looking for fifth or sixth," she said. "The top six were all Russians or Americans, and I saw the difference. And I had a long way to go." She got there the very next year. After finishing fifth at the 2002 Olympics, Suguri made it onto the podium with a bronze medal at the World Championships. It represented, along with Takeshi Honda's bronze earlier in the week, the first Japanese medal at Worlds since Sato's 1994 title. Appropriately, it took place in her home country and in the very city, Nagano, which she had visited four years earlier as a disappointed outsider at the Olympics.

Suguri followed up her big season with an even bigger one in 2002–03, winning two silver medals at fall internationals and qualifying for her first Grand Prix Final. Then she confirmed her position as one of the world's elite, by finishing first in her qualifying group at 2003

Worlds and winning her second straight bronze medal. The only other Japanese woman ever to win medals in consecutive World Championships was Ito in 1989 and 1990.

Suguri's patience and ability to overcome disappointment had paid off. "I guess it doesn't happen right away," she says. Especially with such a late start.

Sarah Hughes

Sarah Hughes figures that success does not come to the timid. And that's why she's the reigning women's Olympic figure skating champion. She set a goal and chased it.

"You've got to grab for it," Hughes said after she won a world bronze medal at the age of 15, the year before she unexpectedly won gold at Salt Lake City. "You can't just be safe. You have to tell everyone you want it."

Hughes practices what she preaches. When she was three years old, she learned to tie her own skate laces so she didn't have to wait for her mother, Amy, to finish with her older children's skates. At five, Sarah could land double toe loops and double Salchows.

When she was six, Hughes wowed a full house with her poise in an ice show at Lake Placid, headlined by Kristi Yamaguchi. At eight, she toured France and Switzerland with world champion ice dancers Maia Usova and Sasha Zhulin. She worked with coach Jeff DiGregorio, a jumping specialist, then moved to Robin Wagner and trained in Hackensack, New Jersey. Before her 13th birthday, Hughes had mastered all five triple jumps used by elite women skaters, and claimed the U.S. Junior Championship.

The next year, at age 13, she won a silver medal at Junior Worlds and finished fourth at U.S. Senior Nationals. It was a stunning achievement but a spot short of a berth on the 1999 world team. But second-place finisher Naomi Nari Nam was even younger than Hughes and the International Skating Union had a rule prohibiting any skater under 15 from Worlds, unless she had won a world Junior medal. So Hughes went to Worlds, her first senior international of any kind. She finished an unexpected seventh, and she wasn't even in high school yet!

Hughes was earning a reputation for pushing the technical envelope. She was doing the triple Salchow/triple loop combinations and was also working on the extremely rare triple loop/triple loop and was practicing triple Axels.

Wagner gave her a more mature freeskate program, Don Quixote, for the 2000–01 season, and Hughes' increased sophistication was immediately evident. She made the podium in all three of her Grand Prix events, finished second at the U.S. Nationals, third at the Grand Prix Final and third at Vancouver, for her first Worlds medal.

"It's been a dream season," she said. But that dream was nothing compared to the fantasy season Hughes

Born: May 2, 1985, Great Neck, New York

Hometown: Great Neck

Training Site: Hackensack, New Jersey

Coach: Robin Wagner

Choreographer: Robin Wagner

RESULTS

2000: 5th Worlds
2nd Sparkassen Cup
2nd Skate America
3rd Cup of Russia

2001: 3rd Worlds
2nd U.S. Nationals
1st Skate Canada
2nd Skate America
2nd Lalique Trophy

2002: 1st Olympics

2003: 6th Worlds

Worlds | Vancouver | March 2001

enjoyed as a 16-year-old in 2001–02. Michelle Kwan and Irina Slutskaya were expected to go head-to-head again for the Olympic gold at Salt Lake City. Hughes, meanwhile, got off to a good start by beating both leading contenders at Skate Canada. But she was only third at the Grand Prix Final, and she finished second to Kwan at U.S. Nationals.

Sarah Hughes was in fourth place after the short program at Salt Lake City. A medal

- When she won her bronze at 2001 Worlds, Sarah was still just a sophomore at Great Neck High School, doing her homework in the car on the long drive to the rink.

Olympics | Salt Lake City | February 2002

seemed tenuous. But just before the Olympics, she and Wagner had improved the program, changing the last 90 seconds of music and adding a second triple-triple combination. Hughes skated onto the ice and told everyone there that she wanted it. She landed both triple-triple combinations, the first time a woman skater had done that. She sailed through the most difficult women's freeskate in Olympic history with exuberance and joy. As she was finishing, the audience jumped to its feet in thunderous appreciation. Hughes had to wait for four more skaters, but most skated tentatively under the enormous pressure, and when it was over Hughes had made the

unlikely leap from fourth to first. At 16, she had become the fourth-youngest Olympic champion.

Hughes embraced the life of Olympic champion, but when the next season rolled around she was a high school senior faced with choices. She had been accepted to Harvard, and other prestigious schools were interested. There was also the call of the professional ranks, as well as the desire to keep on improving at the eligible-skater level, perhaps trying more difficult and daring elements. "I have so many alluring opportunities," she said that winter. "There are so many things I want to do, it's painful to try to think about where I see myself."

Worlds | Washington | March 2003

Olympics | Salt Lake City | February 2002

Hughes suffered from a slightly torn muscle behind her right knee in the fall of 2002, and was unable to compete in the Grand Prix series. Wagner said that the injury, and the agony of choosing a future path, affected her student's dedication to practice. She finished second at Nationals and was entering 2003 Worlds without any international competition since her brilliant skate at Salt Lake City – and without enough serious training time. Hughes struggled through the qualifying round at Worlds, finishing an uncharacteristic sixth in her strong group. She finished sixth overall, the first time she had failed to medal since 2000 Worlds, when she was only 14.

Soon afterward, she decided to forgo the standard summer of touring so she could ponder her future. "I'm a girl with many interests," she said. "The past four years were really geared toward making the Olympic team. That is one of the reasons I was so successful – because I had a goal and stuck to it."

Irina Slutskaya

When she was just a tot, whirling around the family's one-bedroom apartment in Moscow, her grandmother nicknamed her "The Typhoon." Irina Slutskaya hasn't changed much since then.

She is still animated, still full of electricity and still chasing medals.

"When I was in competition for small children I would get flowers, dolls and congratulations," Slutskaya once said. "But I was always crying, 'I want a medal.'" She's got plenty of them, but it wasn't until March 2002 that she got the one she really craved. Three times she had finished second at the World Championships to her old friend and rival Michelle Kwan, but in Nagano, a month after the two of them were overtaken by Sarah Hughes at the Olympics, Slutskaya finally beat Kwan to win the World Championship.

"A couple of times I was just so close and didn't win, and I wondered if it would ever happen," a tearful Slutskaya said after she was presented the elusive gold medal. "And now that it's finally come, I'm just so happy." Slutskaya had been pointed toward the top of the podium for years, and in 2001 she came close when she became the first woman to land a triple-triple-double combination jump at Worlds. But her ferocious athleticism wasn't quite enough to beat Kwan's elegance, and she would have to wait a year for the world title.

The skating world was not treated to another rematch of these titans in 2003 because Slutskaya skipped the World Championships in order to be with her mother, who was battling a serious kidney illness. "I now know that skating isn't the most important thing in life," she said somberly after winning the 2003 European title. That victory, in her last skate of the season, was Slutskaya's fifth European championship, just one short of the record held by two legends, Sonja Henie and Katarina Witt. Both of those women, while remembered more for their style and charisma, made their early impressions in the sport as strong, athletic skaters who burned with the desire to achieve. And Slutskaya is cut from the same cloth.

In 2000 she became the first female to land a triple Lutz/triple loop when she rode the combination to the gold medal at the Grand Prix Final. She also pioneered doing the Biellmann spin first on one foot, then the other. That's the back-arching tulip-shaped spin in which the skater reaches back over her head to grab her skate. With

Born: February 9, 1979, Moscow

Hometown: Moscow

Training Site: Moscow

Coach: Zhanna Gromova

Choreographer: Margarita Romanenko

RESULTS

2000: 2nd Worlds
1st Grand Prix Final
1st Europeans
1st Cup of Russia
1st Russian Nationals
1st NHK

2001: 2nd Worlds
1st Grand Prix Final
1st Europeans
1st Russian Nationals
1st Cup of Russia
1st Skate Canada
1st Goodwill Games

2002: 2nd Olympics
1st Worlds
2nd Europeans
2nd Cup of Russia
2nd Grand Prix Final
2nd NHK

2003: 1st Europeans

Skate Canada | Mississauga
November 2000

- Irina's hobby is collecting stuffed animals. She has more than 200 of them.

all these innovations, Slutskaya has set a new technical standard which, combined with Kwan's artistry, stirred the women's division out of its longtime doldrums.

"Michelle and I have been competing against each other for a long time now. We're good friends, but there

Olympics | Salt Lake City | February 2002

Worlds | Nice | March 2000

Skate Canada | Mississauga | November 2000

can only be one first place," said Slutskaya, who had beaten Kwan twice earlier in the 2001 season. "And I think we've learned from each other."

Slutskaya has certainly learned to be as engaging on the ice as she has always been off it. She burst onto the world scene as an energetic 15-year-old jumper, finishing third to Kwan at the 1994 Junior Worlds, which she won the next season. In 1996, she became the first Russian woman to win the European title, and when she repeated that feat in 1997, it completed Russia's sweep of all four golds, the first time one country had captured all four European titles.

But, despite her successes, she has always skated with an isolated determination, seeming to concentrate more on her jumps than on the audience. That began to change, though, with a skating disaster: her triple Lutz inexplicably

deserted her during the 1998–99 season. After finishing second at the '98 Worlds she could not even make the Russian team for Europeans or Worlds the following year. She considered retiring from the sport.

"It was a shock. I never thought I would drop so fast," she admitted. "I couldn't go five minutes on the ice without crying. I couldn't even watch Worlds on TV."

But in her misery, Slutskaya discovered how much she loved figure skating, and she resumed training with a new energy. She worked on toning her body, paid more attention to the little details of skating, became more fluent in English, switched to choreographer Elena Matveeva, chose more mature programs and, she says, "just grew up." She also married her boyfriend, Sergei Mikheyev, on August 6, 1999.

Her new happiness and emotional stability were

Skate Canada | Mississauga | November 2000

reflected in her skating, and during the 1999–2000 season, she won her first National title, her third European crown and the Grand Prix Final – and was second at Worlds. The stunning comeback set the stage for a renewal of her rivalry with Kwan, which was supposed to culminate at the 2002 Salt Lake City Olympics.

But neither skater won at Salt Lake City. Sarah Hughes rallied to win gold while Slutskaya finished second and Kwan third. But soon the skating world was back to its longest-running rivalry as Slutskaya won the 2002 Worlds and Kwan won in 2003.

Slutskaya's dogged recoveries from the despair of 1998 and an Olympic loss did not surprise those people who knew her best. When she was just four, Slutskaya's mother, Natalia, a teacher and a talented skier in her youth, introduced her daughter to skating at one of Moscow's outdoor rinks. She thought the fresh air would do her good. Soon, Irina started to train with Zhanna Gromova, still the only coach she has ever had.

Gromova recalls the Slutskaya of those early years as "a tiny butterball of energy, all bundled up in layers of clothes, always smiling, always ready to go, always trying." That description could apply almost word-for-word today.

"I have to take my heart into my hands and encourage myself to go on," she says.

She always does.

Elena Sokolova

There were so many years between her silver medals that Elena Sokolova had time to grow up. When the talented 17-year-old finished second at the 1997 World Junior Championships she was tagged as "a great hope for Russian figure skating." But that medal was her last major impact on the skating world until the end of the 2002–03 season, when she finished second at the European Championships and second at Worlds. Sokolova's pair of silvers in 2003 capped a comeback performance that was the biggest shock of the entire skating season. She had been absent from skating's major competitions since finishing eighth at the 1998 Worlds, when she was still heralded as a future contender.

That future looked like it might never arrive, but despite setback after setback Sokolova never gave up. "I won't quit until I start winning," she joked in 2001, one of her worst seasons. "So if you want me to quit, then let me win." Nobody let Sokolova win. She took winning into her own hands when she finally learned how to beat back the nerves that had scuttled her performances since the 1998–99 season, particularly at the highly competitive Russian Nationals, where European and World Championship berths are earned.

She felt her coach, Viktor Kudriavtsev, favored Viktoria Volchkova, and in a desperate effort to find some consistency and success, Sokolova decided to move from her native Moscow in the spring of 1999. She chose the completely different atmosphere of Alexei Mishin's St. Petersburg skating center, where Evgeny Plushenko trains.

Despite the change in training venues, every time she made a mistake she still would have trouble overcoming it – and her programs would unravel. The best she could do was a second at the 2000 Cup of Russia and a victory at the lightly regarded Top Jump competition in 2001.

When she went back to Kudriavtsev in the fall of 2002, Sokolova had become a better all-round skater. "Both of us really changed. We realized we're both part of the whole team," she said of her return. Sokolova won her first Russian championship in 2003, then followed that up with a silver at Europeans.

While everyone was talking about an American women's medal sweep at Worlds, no one really noticed that Sokolova was on a roll. She was the only skater to land two triple-triple combinations in the qualifying round, then did it again in the freeskate final, finishing behind only Michelle Kwan's refined performance. "My coach told me not to leave the ice without a triple-triple combination," she said. "For a long time I couldn't believe that I won the Nationals, but I think that victory instilled confidence in me." And in a performance sport like figure skating, confidence is everything.

Born: February 15, 1980, Moscow

Hometown: Moscow

Training Site: Moscow

Coach: Viktor Kudriavtsev

Choreographer: Alla Kapranova

RESULTS

2000: 6th Russian Nationals
2nd Cup of Russia
1st Finlandia Trophy

2001: 6th Grand Prix Final
4th Russian Nationals
10th Skate America
4th Cup of Russia

2002: 4th Russian Nationals
6th NHK

2003: 2nd Worlds
2nd Europeans
1st Russian Nationals

Worlds | Washington | March 2003

- Elena suffered a concussion in the summer of 2002 and considered retiring, but her mother convinced her to stick with the sport.

Elena Liashenko

If it's difficult for skating fans to understand why some skaters aren't consistent, it's often more difficult for the skaters themselves to figure out.

Elena Liashenko has had competitive results that look like a snakes-and-ladders game board. In 1994, when the Ukraine native was 17, she finished 19th in her first European Championships and 19th again at the Lillehammer Olympics. Yet a month later, she was sixth at Worlds! The next season she won the bronze medal at Europeans, but a year later she was back down to 12th in the world. She missed the Worlds entirely a year after that.

By the 1998–99 season, Liashenko was a top-five skater at Europeans and a solid top-10 finisher at Worlds. Despite starting the season with a serious groin injury, she won her first Grand Prix event, with a shocking gold at Skate Canada '98 in Kamloops, British Columbia. She also made her first Grand Prix Final, "which was really my most important goal of the year," she said. The next season, she was the only woman not from Russia or the United States to qualify for the Grand Prix Final.

"I can't explain it," she said of her improvement. "It just happened by itself. Maybe it's because I am drawing more pleasure from skating. I feel inspired inside. When I was younger, it was much harder for me. Now I understand more and strive toward a goal."

Liashenko grew up in Kiev and began skating when she was four, but the Dinko rink in that city was not the best atmosphere for elite skating. There was no heat and no ice-resurfacing machine. Liashenko was forced to spend four hours a day commuting from home to the rink. When she transferred to the new arena in Kiev in the late 1990s, things improved dramatically.

Liashenko has graduated from the Kiev University of Culture and Sports and works as a sports instructor. She has stabilized herself as a top-eight contender, but has had trouble moving up the ladder into the elite final flight at the World Championships.

"I understand that it will be difficult," she told a skating magazine, "but I believe I can compete for it; if not the top spot at Worlds, then at least a medal. If it doesn't happen this year, then there's next year."

Born: August 9, 1976, Kiev, Ukraine

Hometown: Kiev

Training Site: Kiev

Coach: Marina Amirkhanova

Choreographer: Irina Chubarets

RESULTS

1999: 8th Worlds
7th Europeans
6th Grand Prix Final
2nd Sparkassen Cup
4th NHK

2000: 10th Worlds
5th Europeans
5th Grand Prix Final
4th Sparkassen Cup
6th Cup of Russia

2001: 8th Worlds
4th Europeans

2002: 14th Olympics
6th Worlds
9th Europeans
3rd Skate Canada
4th Lalique Trophy

2003: 7th Worlds
5th Grand Prix Final
5th Europeans

Olympics | Nagano | February 1998

- Elena is one of the most mature competitors in international skating. She says she can't remember a time when she didn't skate.

Worlds | Washington | March 2003

Jennifer Robinson

You're not getting older, you're getting better. It's an advertising slogan from another era, but it fits current star Jennifer Robinson perfectly. "I'm one of the oldest in the event, but I guess I'm a late bloomer; it's taken me a while to hit my stride," an elated Robinson said after she finished second in her qualifying round at the 2003 Worlds and made it to the final flight in the short program, for the first time in her long career. She went on to finish ninth overall, her second straight top-10 finish, capping a strong season when she landed her first triple-triple combination, won her fifth straight Canadian title and broke away from her traditional ballet-style choreography and into a flamenco.

Robinson has won six Canadian Senior Championships overall, setting a record for the modern age. Only Constance Wilson-Samuel, who won nine in a less- demanding era between 1924 and 1935, stood at the top of the podium more often.

It has not been all garlands for Robinson, who has often had to recover from disappointing setbacks by simply working harder. After qualifying for two World Championships and winning the 1996 Canadian title, she suffered through two dismal Nationals in succession, missing the world team in both 1997 and 1998. She had to overcome a tendency to land her triple jumps on two feet during times of stress. And after skyrocketing from 18th at the 1999 Worlds to eighth in her breakthrough season of 2000, she dropped back to 15th the next year. So, although she obviously wants to climb higher, successive ninth-place finishes at Worlds and a gratifying seventh at the 2002 Olympics were welcome signs that she has reserved her own seat at the elite table.

In a discipline filled with short teenagers, Robinson is a tall woman. Using that maturity, height and Robinson's natural grace, choreographer Lori Nichol designs lyrical programs that emphasize her elegance and

Born: December 2, 1976, Goderich, Ontario

Hometown: Windsor, Ontario

Training Site: Barrie, Ontario

Coaches: Michelle Leigh, Doug Leigh

Choreographer: Lori Nichol

RESULTS

2000: 8th Worlds
6th Four Continents
4th Skate Canada
5th Lalique Trophy

2001: 15th Worlds
8th Four Continents
5th Cup of Russia

2002: 7th Olympics
9th Worlds
4th Four Continents
4th Skate Canada
4th Bofrost Cup

2003: 9th Worlds
5th Four Continents

- Jennifer married Mariposa Skating Club coach Shane Dennison in December 2002.

- Jennifer won her first Grand Prix medal in 1999 when she was third at Skate Canada.

Worlds | Nice | March 2000

strong body lines. Robinson is as gracious off the ice as she is graceful on it. She is well aware that if she skates well, as she did in 2002 and 2003, Canada qualifies a second woman for Worlds, often a youngster needing the experience and exposure.

But it's not just that, or her string of titles and medals, that has kept Robinson competing into her mid-20s and beyond. "I love to perform, and this is the best day job," she says. "I love it so much. I want to make sure that I stay a bit too long, so I don't leave anything behind me that I wanted to do."

Viktoria Volchkova

The power of radio is responsible for creating one of the bright stars in the constellation of superb Russian skaters.

Viktoria Volchkova's parents heard a radio announcement about figure skating lessons and took their six-year-old daughter to a rink in St. Petersburg (then Leningrad). Volchkova showed an aptitude for jumping, and because of the fertile history of pairs at the famous Yubileny Rink, she wanted to skate pairs. But she was considered too tall and was put in singles, which was also agreeable because her idol was Oksana Baiul, the 1994 Olympic singles champion.

Eventually Volchkova moved to Moscow to train with Viktor Kudriavtsev, who would help her work her way through the extraordinarily competitive women's ranks in Russia. At 16 she finished third at Junior Worlds, behind two other Russian Juniors! And with Maria Butyrskaya and Irina Slutskaya both still on the scene, it was becoming very crowded at the top of the Russian women's pyramid.

"Russian Nationals are like a minefield," says Volchkova. "There is a lot of pressure; any mistake can be fatal."

Volchkova won the Junior Grand Prix Final in 1999 and also qualified for her first Europeans and Worlds by finishing third at Russian Senior Nationals. She went on to win her first of four straight European bronze medals.

Born: July 30, 1982, St. Petersburg, Russia

Hometown: St. Petersburg

Training Site: Chicago

Coach: Oleg Vasiliev

Choreographers: Elena Matveeva, Alexander Zhulin

RESULTS

2000: 6th Worlds
3rd Europeans
6th Grand Prix Final
4th Skate America
5th Cup of Russia
2nd Lalique Trophy
3rd Russian Nationals

2001: 6th Worlds
3rd Europeans
2nd Russian Nationals

2002: 9th Olympics
7th Worlds
3rd Europeans
3rd Skate Canada
6th Skate America
1st Cup of Russia

2003: 5th Worlds
8th Europeans
3rd Grand Prix Final

Worlds | Washington | March 2003

Volchkova finished a credible 10th in her World Championship debut in 1999, and moved up to sixth for the next two years.

In the spring of 2002, she left Russia to train with former world pairs champion Oleg Vasiliev in Chicago. A few months later she won her first Grand Prix gold medal at Cup of Russia.

She has studied at the Institute for Physical Culture, and is considering a future career in journalism. Perhaps one day it will be her voice on radio, inspiring parents to register their young children in figure skating.

• Viktoria was the first woman to finish third at Europeans for four straight years.

Skate Canada | Quebec City | October 2002

Yoshie Onda

The battle to capture the American title has always been considered the most fierce domestic competition in women's figure skating. But recently, the most intense national struggle just may be the one to determine who is the most promising female skater in Japan.

Like the famous Midori Ito, Yoshie Onda was raised in Nagoya, trains with coach Michiko Yamada, and is acutely focused on landing a triple Axel. When Onda took gold at the Bofrost Cup on Ice in the autumn of 2002, she became the first Japanese female to win a Grand Prix event. (In Ito's and Yuka Sato's eras, fall internationals weren't united into a formal Grand Prix circuit as they are now.) Just to prove that the victory was no fluke, Onda also won the NHK Trophy on home ice a few weeks later.

But aside from Grand Prix victories, there was another crown at stake: the race to become the first woman in the world to land a triple Axel since Ito performed the three-and-a-half rotation jump at the Albertville Olympics in 1992. Onda had spent most of the 2001–02 season attempting, and missing, the difficult element. In fact, she had been accused of concentrating too much on the Axel at the expense of other segments of her skating. But Onda is one of the hardest-working skaters in the world. And beginning with the 2001–02 season, the extra effort she put into improving her carriage and line began earning her improved marks for presentation, which had always been her drawback. "I'm ready to overcome any difficulty," she vowed.

One of those difficulties was that two other young skaters – Yukari Nakano of Japan and Ludmila Nelidina of Russia – landed triple Axels at Skate America 2002. That was only two weeks before Onda won the Bofrost Cup, and came the closest she'd ever come to landing the Axel. Still, she refuses to stop trying. An ankle injury kept her out of the Grand Prix Final and Four Continents in 2003, and contributed directly to her disappointing 11th-place finish at 2003 Worlds, when the planned triple Axel was landed as a double. A year earlier, she had been fifth at Worlds.

Onda has enormous height on her jumps and superb athletic ability. She was still a Junior when she was named

Born:	December 13, 1982, Aichi, Japan
Hometown:	Nagoya
Training Site:	Nagoya
Coach:	Michiko Yamada
Choreographers:	David Wilson, Mihoko Higuchi

RESULTS

2000: 12th Worlds
5th Four Continents
4th Japanese Nationals
8th NHK

2001: 5th Grand Prix Final
3rd Four Continents
2nd Sparkassen Cup
2nd NHK

2002: 7th Olympics
5th Worlds
1st Bofrost Cup
1st NHK

2003: 11th Worlds
2nd Japanese Nationals

Worlds | Washington | March 2003

to the Japanese team for the 2000 World Championships. She finished a commendable 12th, but was hard on herself afterward. "I cracked under pressure," she said. "It made it difficult to attack the programs." And when she attacks programs she is at her best, just as Ito was.

- Yoshie was allowed to miss the 2002 Japanese Nationals and was given a spot on the Olympic team when she qualified for the Grand Prix Final and won the bronze medal at Four Continents.

Jennifer Kirk

She is as graceful as a ballerina, which she once was, but there is a lot of plain fight in **Jennifer Kirk.** She fought to overcome a late start in skating. She had to battle through the tragedy of losing her mother to breast cancer. She left her long-time coaches in Boston because she needed more intensity in her training.

Kirk is one of the top figure skaters in the United States, but that wasn't her original ambition. She was an elite gymnast until she was nine years old and lost her taste for the sport. That autumn she took some figure skating lessons, and found she was well behind the other girls. So she fought to catch up. And within two years she was landing triple jumps. By the age of 14, she was the third-ranked Junior skater in the United States. In 2000, she won the World Junior Championship and, despite being only 15 years old, she finished seventh in the white-hot atmosphere of the U.S. Senior Nationals. She became a regular on the Grand Prix circuit that fall, and won her first senior medal with a bronze at the Lalique Trophy in France.

Kirk solidified her reputation as a future world force when she won the "pewter medal" (fourth place) at the 2001 U.S. Nationals. Seven months later her mother, Patricia, succumbed to breast cancer. "I dedicated that season to my mother," she said. "I wanted to win another big competition in her memory." Although she had a number of strong international finishes, she had to wait until the 2002 Four Continents Championship for the victory that would honor her mother.

She was also named to the U.S. world team, despite finishing only fifth at Nationals, because Olympic champion Sarah Hughes was not going to Worlds and alternate Angela Nikodinov was injured. Before Worlds, however, Kirk left her veteran coaches Mary and Evy Scotveld and moved to Michigan to work with Richard Callaghan. "I wanted a coach with a lot of energy," Kirk explained. Callaghan, who had coached Tara Lipinski to an Olympic title, certainly has energy. At the 2002 Worlds, Kirk was forced to withdraw after the short program when ill-fitting boots aggravated a recurring hip injury. She finished fifth

Born:	August 15, 1984, Newton, Massachusetts
Hometown:	Newton
Training Site:	Rochester Hills, Michigan
Coach:	Richard Callaghan
Choreographer:	Olga Volozhinskaya

RESULTS

2000: 1st World Juniors
7th U.S. Nationals
3rd Lalique Trophy
6th NHK

2001: 5th Four Continents
4th U.S. Nationals
4th Nations Cup

2002: 1st Four Continents
5th U.S. Nationals
4th Skate America
6th Skate Canada

2003: 5th U.S. Nationals

- Jennifer has performed in the Boston Ballet's *Nutcracker Suite* four times.

- Jennifer started gymnastics at age five and was a level nine competitor until she left the sport when she was nine to take up figure skating.

- In her first year as a senior, Jennifer was landing a triple Lutz/triple toe loop combination

SkateAmerica | Spokane | October 2002

again at U.S. Nationals in 2003. But with Callaghan working on her spins and increasing the height of her jumps and Olga Volozhinskaya providing interesting choreography, the buzz is that Kirk can't be held off the podium much longer. She has far too much fight for that.

Joannie Rochette

It was a season that wasn't even supposed to begin, but it ended with Joannie Rochette on the same warmup ice as her all-time role model. The walls of Rochette's bedroom in Berthierville, Quebec, are adorned with posters of the world's best skaters, including Michelle Kwan. So it was understandable that Rochette was a little in awe when her qualifying round flight at her first World Championships (2003 in Washington) also included Kwan. "It was like a dream for me," she said. "I shouldn't have, but I was watching her on the ice. I saw how she was at ease with the audience and in the warmup, and I can learn from that."

Rochette probably shouldn't have even been at those Worlds. In the fall, she was advised by doctors to stay off the ice for four months because of a stress fracture in her right leg. Her parents recommended that she try a bone regeneration machine, and it helped overcome the injury. But she still missed 10 weeks of critical training time. She was forced to skip NHK and Lalique Trophy, the first two Grand Prix assignments of her career. Because of the down time, Rochette wasn't even considering a repeat of her performance at 2002 Canadians, when she was the surprise bronze medal winner. "I kind of forgot about that," she said.

But she didn't forget how to skate, and in just her second year of Senior competition she won the silver medal at 2003 Canadians – to earn a berth on the world team. After a respectable eighth-place finish at Four Continents, Rochette suffered a number of falls in the freeskate and finished in 17th place. "I'm really mad about that," she said, with determination. "It will help my motivation and I'll try harder not to have this happen again."

Rochette has already shown that she can rebound quickly from a setback. The woman some Canadian skating officials are calling "The Next One" finished 15th in the 1999 Canadian Novice Championships, when she was 13. The next year she won the title. The season after that she won the Canadian Junior Championship and in another year she was collecting the bronze in Senior. "She's very quick," says Canadian skating guru Louis Stong. "And there is something whimsical and charming about her." There's something very tough about her, too.

Born: January 13, 1986, Montreal, Quebec

Hometown: Berthierville, Quebec

Training Site: Montreal

Coach: Manon Perron

Choreographer: David Wilson

RESULTS

2000: 1st Canadian Novice Championships
5th St. Gervais
4th Mexico Cup
2nd Mladost Trophy

2001: 8th World Juniors
1st Canadian Juniors
5th Gdansk Junior Grand Prix
3rd Milan Junior Grand Prix

2002: 9th Four Continents
5th World Juniors
3rd Canadian Nationals

2003: 17th World Championships
8th Four Continents
2nd Canadian Nationals

Canadians | Saskatoon | January 2003

- Joannie landed her first triple, the Salchow, at age 12.

- Joannie does a difficult triple toe loop/half-loop/triple Salchow sequence.

THE
PAIRS
TEAMS

Xue Shen and Hongbo Zhao

Maria Petrova and Alexei Tikhonov

Tatiana Totmianina and Maxim Marinin

Tiffany Scott and Philip Dulebohn

Anabelle Langlois and Patrice Archetto

Sarah Abitbol and Stephane Bernadis

Elizabeth Putnam and Sean Wirtz

Dorota Zagorska and Mariusz Siudek

Yuko Kawaguchi and Alexander Markuntsov

Rena Inoue and John Baldwin

Just when it appeared that there was a serious decline in pairs interest around the world, there has been a recent revival. The three countries with the most skating depth – Canada, Russia and the United States – are still the driving forces in pairs. But other countries, particularly China, are discovering, and mastering, the discipline.

Inspired by two-time world champions Xue Shen and Hongbo Zhao, the Chinese are taking pairs so seriously that they provided the top five finishers in the pairs event at the 2001 Junior Grand Prix Finals. China and Russia took the top four spots at the 2003 Worlds, with Shen and Zhao unequaled in a majestic freeskate that would have been championship caliber in any era. Qing Pang and Jai Tong finished fourth and

could be medal-bound. And the sixth-place duo of Dan Zhang and Hao Zhang has caught everyone's eye.

Zhang and Zhang are not related – except in their athletic partnership, which produced a dazzling quadruple twist at the 2000 World Junior Championships. The quad twist, in which the woman is thrown straight above the partner roughly parallel to the ice and rotates four times, is one of the sport's most visually effective tricks and had rarely been attempted since the early career of Russian legends Ekaterina Gordeeva and the late Sergei Grinkov in the 1980s. They're doing triples in Seniors, but the quad is sure to follow soon.

In France, a long-dormant pairs interest has been reawakened by the 2000 World bronze won by Sarah Abitbol and Stephane Bernadis, who've been injury-plagued

ever since but are still on the world scene. Even Japan, with little of a pairs tradition, has an interesting pair in Yuko Kawaguchi and Russian-trained Alexander Markuntsov. And Canada, which had expected to spend a few years rebuilding after Olympic co-champions Jamie Salé and David Pelletier turned professional, is suddenly thrust right back into the picture with an unexpected fifth-place finish at 2003 Worlds by Anabelle Langlois and Patrice Archetto. And there's plenty of backup, particularly from the new pair of Elizabeth Putnam and Sean Wirtz, who finished third at Nationals.

At the World Championships from 1998 through 2003, seven different countries were represented on the pairs podium. At the Salt Lake City Olympics, there were six active pairs who'd won world medals.

But what people will always remember about pairs skating at the 2002 Games was the worst scandal to rock figure skating in its 106-year history of elite competitions. Four days after the actual final, Canadian pair Jamie Salé and David Pelletier and Russian team Elena Berezhnaya and Anton Sikharulidze were both awarded gold medals after the French judge confessed to being pressured into voting for the Russians over the Canadians. That vote had been just enough to originally give the gold medal to Berezhnaya and Sikharulidze. The incident has cast a long shadow over figure skating that will not lift for years, and it overshadowed how far those two pairs had elevated the discipline beyond its former technical and artistic limits.

There have been various stages of pairs skating over the past quarter-century, shifting from an emphasis on side-by-side jumps in the early 1980s, to huge throws, and then to complex lifts. But recent champions have also evoked a musical unison, intense inter-partner chemistry and a dancelike choreography in the genre. With a post-Olympic changing of the guard to less experienced teams (outside of Shen and Zhao), that process has been stalled a bit, but it should be back on track well before the 2006 Olympics.

It is harder to bring seamless, emotional choreography to pairs than to any other discipline. Essentially, pairs skating is freeskating performed in unison. The partners' movements are supposed to be synchronized, whether they are together or apart. But because the man must be big enough to throw his partner great distances, and the woman must be small enough to be aerodynamic, it's difficult to get the right physical match so that their lines are in harmony. And when one partner is trying complicated tasks while dupli-

cating, or mirroring, the exact movements of the other, it's often too much to demand that they also connect with passion. But that's what the top pairs are expected to do. There is also a huge fear factor.

No job in figure skating, and few in any sport, is more dangerous than being a pairs skater. The woman must be courageous because she is being propelled for distances of up to 20 feet, or held aloft by one hand of a partner who is doing turns. The man is constantly in danger of his head and face being sliced during the extremely complicated new dismounts from lifts. So pairs skaters must be of the right build, technically accomplished enough to land triple jumps, brave enough to handle the potential for serious injury, trained well enough to match their partner's movements, and collected enough to demonstrate an emotional connection between them.

In all, there are so many complex requirements, it's no wonder many countries simply can't find enough skaters to build a strong pairs program. And it's no wonder that the stronger skating nations are exporting pairs skaters to other countries.

Xue Shen & Hongbo Zhao

Nearly every year, Xue Shen and Hongbo Zhao add another item to their long list of "firsts."

The dynamic pairs team, who have arguably the best throws in the history of the sport, were the first Chinese pair to win a major international event, when they captured NHK in 1997. They were the winners of the first Four Continents Championships, held at Halifax in 1999. That was also the first ISU Championship ever won by a Chinese pair. That same season they became the first Chinese pair to win a world medal, with their silver at Worlds in Helsinki. And in 2000, they won the Grand Prix Final, the first Chinese skaters to do that.

The fleet-footed couple have become the trendsetters for a growing legion of Chinese pairs. But when Shen and Zhao were starting out, they had no role models to imitate.

Shen and Zhao are both from the northern city of Harbin, often called the coldest city in China. There were two rinks, but only one of them was heated, and the ice was far harder than figure skaters like it because the arenas were also used for speed skating and hockey.

Shen was a somewhat frail child, and her parents registered her in skating at the age of eight in the hopes that she would grow stronger. She began her career as a singles skater.

Zhao, whose father is a violinist and mother is a worker in a textile factory, started skating when he was six. He was playing basketball when skating coach Bin Yao noticed how well he moved and suggested he take up skating. Zhao was partnered with Maomao Xie and finished 11th at Junior Worlds, but in 1992 Yao decided to break up the pair and teamed Zhao with Shen. He was 18 and she was only 13.

Although Yao had skated pairs internationally (finishing 15th at 1980 Worlds, the first time China competed in pairs), there wasn't much history of the discipline in China. So Zhao and Shen studied videotapes of the world's top

Born: November 13, 1978, Harbin, China; September 22, 1973, Harbin

Hometown: Harbin

Training Site: Beijing

Coach: Bin Yao

Choreographers: Tatiana Tarasova, Lea Ann Miller

RESULTS

2000: 2nd Worlds
2nd Skate America
2nd Cup of Russia
1st NHK

2001: 3rd Worlds
2nd Four Continents
1st Chinese Nationals
1st Sparkassen Cup
1st NHK

2002: 3rd Olympics
1st Worlds
1st Bofrost Cup
1st Cup of Russia
1st NHK

2003: 1st Worlds
2nd Grand Prix Final
1st Four Continents

Worlds | Vancouver
March 2001

- Xue and Hongbo regularly land throw quad jumps in practice.

- After each competition, Xue and Hongbo meticulously analyze every part of their programs, to see where they can improve for the next event.

teams, dissecting every move. In their second season together they won the national championship and, in

Worlds | Vancouver | March 2001

Worlds | Washington | March 2003

1994, entered their first Worlds, finishing a distant 21st. From there, they began one of the longest climbs to the podium in pairs history. After a year off because of an injury to Zhao, they returned to finish 15th at 1996 Worlds.

The pair always drew attention because of how far, and how high, Zhao heaved the fearless Shen in their pairs throws. They were also very competent individual jumpers. But they struggled with other elements such as spins and lifts. And there was very little true unison on the ice.

But Shen and Zhao were eager students and kept working at their shortcomings. They won their first international at NHK in 1997, and a few months later their

magnificent athleticism carried them to fourth place at the 1998 Worlds, seven spots better than the previous year.

They followed that up with their Four Continents win in 1999 and a controversial runner-up finish to reigning world champions Elena Berezhnaya and Anton Sikharulidze at the 1999 Worlds in Helsinki. Shen and Zhao received the only standing ovation of the freeskate, and many observers – including several of their opponents – thought the Chinese were the best pair in that competition.

Shen and Zhao had spent time training in Russia and in Simsbury, Connecticut, so they weren't shy about seeking international help. Because their presentation marks

Olympics | Salt Lake City | February 2002

were holding them back, in 1999 they came to prominent Toronto choreographer Sandra Bezic, who works with several skaters and is also the creative director for Stars on Ice, the world's leading professional show. Respected American choreographer Michael Siebert also took part in the sessions. In recent years, the skaters have been choreographed by Tatiana Tarasova and Lea Ann Miller.

"Everything was new to them – the concept of choreography, the way we worked. They didn't grow up with any of this," said Bezic, who had to speak to the pair through an interpreter. They slowly began to overcome their three shortcomings: spins, overall artistry and on-ice connection. They won a silver at 2000 Worlds despite missing a month of training when Shen broke her nose in a practice session. But they had it together by the Grand Prix Final, which they won, and Worlds.

For the 2000–01 season, Shen and Zhao added a second side-by-side triple jump. And at Worlds, on what may have been the finest night of pairs skating ever, they won the bronze medal. And they put it all together to win gold at 2002 Worlds. It appeared they might not be able to defend their title when Shen hurt her right knee and ankle practicing a throw quadruple Salchow. They considered withdrawing but rallied to win the 2003 title with a brilliantly seamless freeskate. Said awed commentator Debi Wilkes, "It is almost as if they have no skates on."

Just as they've done throughout their careers.

Worlds | Washington | March 2003

Marina Petrova
& Alexei Tikhonov

When your country has captured all but six of the last 35 world pairs championships, the expectations feel like a block of cement on your shoulders. But in March 2000 Marina Petrova and Alexei Tikhonov withstood the immense pressure to provide Russia with its usual reward.

Petrova and Tikhonov weren't the favorites among the world's top pairs. They weren't even the favorites among their own country's top pairs. That label was worn by two-time world champions Elena Berezhnaya and Anton Sikharulidze. But when she tested positive for banned ingredients in a cough syrup, the pair forfeited their European title to Petrova and Tikhonov. Berezhnaya and Sikharulidze also dropped out of the World Championships in Nice, France, leaving Petrova and Tikhonov with the burden of continuing Russian dominance.

While the rest of the field struggled, their acrobatic lifts and throws carried them to the world title, just 21 months after they formed their partnership.

It was a long and winding road, filled with other partners and lots of medals, that led to Petrova and Tikhonov's union. Ironically, Petrova first attracted international attention skating with Sikharulidze. They won the 1994 and 1995 World Junior Championships together. But Sikharulidze was determined to skate with Berezhnaya, and he left Petrova in 1996. Petrova then paired with Teimaruz Pulin for two years, and they won a silver medal at the 1997 Junior Worlds. That partnership didn't have much spark, and when Pulin eventually developed health problems, Petrova called Tikhonov.

Petrova and Tikhonov were fourth in their first Worlds, but in their sophomore season they won three Grand Prix events and capped off the year with their World Championship. With their coach Ludmila Velikova, they continue to improvise, especially on their lifts. "We get new ideas," Petrova says. "And we're always working on them."

🌐 Worlds | Washington | March 2003

Born: November 29, 1977 St. Petersburg, Russia; November 1, 1971, Samara, Russia

Hometown: St. Petersburg

Training Site: St. Petersburg

Coach: Ludmila Velikova

Choreographer: Sergei Petukhov

Skate Canada | Mississauga
November 2000

RESULTS

2000: 1st Worlds
1st Europeans

2001: 4th Worlds
4th Europeans
2nd Cup of Russia
2nd NHK

2002: 6th Olympics
4th Worlds
3rd Europeans
2nd Cup of Russia
4th NHK

2003: 3rd Worlds
3rd Grand Prix Final
3rd Europeans

• Marina and Alexei have won a world title and two European Championships. But they've never finished first at Russian Nationals.

Tatiana Totmianina & Maxim Marinin

Play to your strengths and work on your weaknesses. That may be a basic formula for steady advancement in elite figure skating, but it's much easier said than done.

Because they both said it and did it, Tatiana Totmianina and Maxim Marinin have moved to within one step of the world pairs skating championship. The Russian pair won silver medals at both the 2002 and 2003 Worlds after spending the earlier part of their careers making serious changes. But they never forgot what got them together in the first place: similar, strong jumping techniques.

They began their careers as singles skaters. Totmianina lived in St. Petersburg and competed in the women's division until 1996, when she and Marinin teamed up. Marinin had moved into pairs after he was beaten by Evgeny Plushenko, who was five years younger, in a competition in Volgograd, where both young men grew up.

For the first five years of their partnership, Totmianina and Marinin trained in St. Petersburg with coach Natalia Pavlova. But just before making a major breakthrough with a silver medal at the 2001 Europeans, the pair split with their coach. So they made another major change and, after Europeans, moved to Chicago to work with Oleg Vasiliev, the 1984 Olympic pairs champion who was gaining a reputation as a coach.

Vasiliev was unable to accompany Totmianina and Marinin to Worlds, where they finished in fifth place. But they were beginning to create their own light instead of living in the shadow of two other Russian teams who had won world titles: Maria Petrova and Alexei Tikhonov, and Elena Berezhnaya and Anton Sikharulidze. As Marinin explained, "We needed to do something better than the other Russian pairs. If you do the same, nobody sees you." Because of their background in singles, that "something better" was jumping, and they were among the first pairs to incorporate consistently two triple jumps (the toe loop and Salchow) into their programs, even doing one of them in combination.

They are a sleek, fast team, but had to improve themselves at the more visually impressive pairs elements – lifts and spins – and boost their overall presentation. As they began to do that under Vasiliev's tutelage, the medals started coming by the armful.

They won their first European Championship in 2002,

Born: November 2, 1981, Perm, Russia
March 23, 1977, Volgograd

Hometown: St. Petersburg

Training Site: Chicago

Coach: Oleg Vasiliev

Choreographers:
Svetlana Korol, Giuseppe Arena

RESULTS

2001: 5th Worlds
2nd Europeans
2nd Skate Canada
3rd Skate America
4th Lalique Trophy

2002: 4th Olympics
2nd Worlds
1st Europeans
1st Skate America
1st Skate Canada
1st Lalique Trophy

2003: 2nd Worlds
1st Grand Prix Final
1st Europeans

Olympics | Salt Lake City
February 2002

then just missed the podium at the Olympics, before taking silver at Worlds. That strong finish spilled over into a brilliant 2002–03 season. They were undefeated all season before having to settle for second place at Worlds behind the brilliant freeskate of Xue Shen and Hongbo Zhao. They may not yet be world champions, but they no longer skate in anyone's shadow.

• Tatiana and Maxim have tried, unsuccessfully, to land side-by-side triple Lutzes in competition. For now, they've abandoned that quest.

Tiffany Scott & Philip Dulebohn

After test-driving their partnership for a week, Tiffany Scott thought she would try skating with Philip Dulebohn, "just for the summer."

They must have long summers in Delaware. Eight years later, Scott and Dulebohn were still together and had finished in Worlds' top 10 three times.

In 2003, after winning their first U.S. Seniors title, they finished ninth at Worlds, the same spot they held in 2000. They were seventh in 2002, up six spots from a disappointing Olympics.

In the beginning, even qualifying for the Worlds seemed to be out of the question. At their first junior regional competition, Scott and Dulebohn placed last among the five entrants, the kind of discouraging result that can lead to a quick breakup.

"We had a rough start," Scott concedes. "It took us a while to click."

But they had faith in each other and stuck it out. They got along well together, and they are strong individual skaters because each had experience in singles. Their confidence in the partnership was rewarded with a bronze medal at the 1997 Junior Nationals.

"That was a big moment," Dulebohn agrees. "We proved ourselves that day."

They kept proving themselves, eventually jumping onto the U.S. Seniors podium with a silver medal in 2000, immediately followed by a bronze at Four Continents. That foreshadowed their breakthrough into the top 10 at Worlds.

"I don't think people anticipated our getting to this point when we started," Dulebohn said.

His partner hadn't even anticipated getting past the summer.

Born: May 1, 1977, Weymouth, Massachusetts; September 13, 1973, Silver Springs, Maryland

Hometowns: Hanson, Massachusetts; Germantown, Maryland

Training Site: Newark, Delaware

Coach: Karl Kurtz

Choreographers: Karl Kurtz, Gorsha Sur, Rene Roca

RESULTS

1999: 6th Four Continents
6th Skate America
6th Lalique Trophy
5th U.S. Nationals

2000: 9th Worlds
3rd Four Continents
8th Cup of Russia
2nd U.S. Nationals

2001: 11th Worlds
3rd Four Continents
2nd U.S. Nationals

2002: 13th Olympics
7th Worlds
5th Skate Canada
5th Lalique Trophy

2003: 9th Worlds
5th Four Continents
1st U.S. Nationals

Four Continents | Salt Lake City | February 2001

- Tiffany started skating at age four, while Philip was five when he took to the ice.

- Philip was a single who skated internationally as a junior.

- Philip's brother, Paul, was a nationally ranked pairs and singles skater. He now coaches.

Anabelle Langlois & Patrice Archetto

Canada has such a rich tradition of pairs skating that even the retirement of an Olympic Championship team did not create panic. Eventually, another pair was bound to challenge for the world podium. What Canadians didn't realize was that it could happen so soon.

When Jamie Salé and David Pelletier turned professional after their gold medal at the 2002 Olympics, there were three or four potential successors. Jacinthe Larivière and Lenny Faustino won the vacant national title, but Anabelle Langlois and Patrice Archetto were the pair that began to fill the void on the international scene.

After a respectable 12th-place finish at the 2002 Olympics, Langlois and Archetto temporarily moved to Edmonton from Montreal to train for the World Championships. With help from Jan Ullmark – the coach who put the finishing touches on Salé and Pelletier – they finished a strong 10th at Worlds. So they left Montreal and coach Josée Picard and made a permanent switch to Ullmark. In Edmonton they got plenty of input from Salé and Pelletier, and the advice paid off during 2002–03.

Langlois and Archetto finished fifth at the 2003 Worlds, a spectacular result that caught everyone except the two skaters off-guard.

Langlois was a nationally ranked singles skater in Novice and didn't try pairs skating until she was 15. Two years later, in 1998, she teamed up with Archetto after his mother, a skating judge, had noticed Langlois' combination of jumping ability and courage.

Langlois and Archetto were not an instant success. They finished eighth in the divisional championships in their first

Born: July 21, 1982, Grand-Mère, Quebec; March 12, 1972, Montreal

Hometowns: Hull, Quebec; Montreal

Training Site: Edmonton, Alberta

Coach: Jan Ullmark

Choreographer: Nikolai Morozov

RESULTS

2001: 6th Four Continents
3rd Canadian Nationals
3rd Skate Canada

2002: 12th Olympics
10th Worlds
2nd Four Continents
3rd Canadian Nationals
2nd Skate America
3rd Skate Canada
3rd NHK

2003: 5th Worlds
6th Grand Prix Final
4th Four Continents
2nd Canadian Nationals

Skate America | Spokane
October 2002

year and ninth at Nationals in their second. But in 2001, they had improved enough to win a bronze medal at the Canadian Championships. They won a second bronze a year later.

The next year, with a new coach and with more sophisticated choreography designed by ice dance specialist Nikolai Morozov, they won three medals on the circuit and were the only Canadians to qualify for the Grand Prix Final. They had a poor freeskate at Nationals and finished second, but more than made up for that with a spectacular freeskate at Worlds, which moved them from sixth place to fifth.

Once again, the future of Canadian pairs skating was in safe hands.

- Patrice trained to be a firefighter. As a child, Anabelle traveled around the world with her parents.

- "He's very calm and I'm up and down," Anabelle says of Patrice. "We complete each other very well."

Sarah Abitbol & Stephane Bernadis

The tradition of pairs skating in France is like the tradition of sun-tanning at the North Pole. There isn't one.

When Sarah Abitbol and Stephane Bernadis powered their way to a bronze medal at the 2000 Worlds, it was the first world pairs medal for France in 68 years. What made the 2000 medal more remarkable was that the day before, Bernadis had his left forearm slashed by an unknown assailant in the doorway of his hotel room. He received four stitches in the arm and was surrounded by heavy security – an emotionally draining experience. The excitement seemed to suit a couple known for their dramatic approach to the sport. They have often been compared with ice dancers for their artistry and expression.

Abitbol took to the ice at six. She liked pairs but also skated singles, finishing 21st at Junior Worlds in 1993. Bernadis's mother, Donna Davies, was a former member of the British national skating team, and she encouraged her eight-year-old son to take up the sport. He decided upon pairs because he didn't think he'd succeed in singles. Abitbol and Bernadis got together at a tryout camp in 1992. And by 1994, they had won their first of 10 consecutive French Championships.

Their victory total ties the national record of Andrée Joly and Pierre Brunet, the last French pairs legends, who won world titles in the 1920s and '30s. But the athletic pair, whose specialty is throw jumps, missed two consecutive World Championships because of injury after winning bronze on "home" ice at Nice in 2000. In 2002, Abitbol tore her left Achilles tendon in practice. Not only did the couple miss the Olympics, but Abitbol was off the ice completely for six months.

With little training time under their belts, Abitbol and Bernadis won their seventh medal (silver) at Europeans in

Born: June 8, 1976, Nantes, France; February 23, 1974, Boulogne Billancourt

Hometowns: Paris, Bougival

Training Site: Paris

Coach: Jean-Christophe Simond

Choreographer: Tatiana Tarasova

RESULTS

2000: 3rd Worlds
3rd Europeans
1st Sparkassen Cup
4th Lalique Trophy
2nd NHK

2001: 3rd Europeans
5th Grand Prix Final
3rd Cup of Russia
3rd Lalique Trophy

2002: 2nd Europeans
6th Grand Prix Final
2nd Lalique Trophy

2003: 12th Worlds
2nd Europeans

- In the summer of 1992 Bernadis teamed with Surya Bonaly, but she decided to concentrate on singles (very successfully).

- Abitbol began skating at school at six, when she had to choose between that sport and swimming for physical education.

2003. Before Worlds they switched coaches from Stanislav Leonovich to former singles star Jean-Christophe Simond. They finished only 12th at Worlds, but it was still a satisfying comeback season. "It was hard for me to imagine 10 months ago that I would even participate," Abitbol said.

Elizabeth Putnam & Sean Wirtz

You have only one chance to make a first impression, and Elizabeth Putnam and Sean Wirtz made the most of theirs. Their debut at the 2003 Canadian Championships produced a surprise bronze medal for Putnam and Wirtz, who had been together only six months.

Every once in a while a new pairs combination is just right, and the skating world sits up and takes notice. It happened with Jamie Salé and David Pelletier, who had both been veterans of the Canadian singles and pairs scene before forming one of the most remarkable, and mercurial, pairs teams of recent years. Many observers had the same stirrings about Putnam and Wirtz in their debut season.

The audience's eyes are immediately drawn to Putnam and Wirtz because of the skaters' long lines and understanding of edges – which they put to good use with visually impressive side-by-side spread eagles and spiral sequences. And they include two side-by-side triple jumps in their programs. Both partners are strong singles skaters, which helps explain their quick start as a pairs team. In fact, in 2003 Putnam not only won a bronze medal with Wirtz at Canadian Nationals, but also, on the very same day, won a bronze medal in junior women's singles.

Putnam finished ninth in senior pairs with Mark Batka in 2002. "I definitely prefer pairs to singles, though," she says. "The throws and lifts are a lot of fun." Wirtz won the Canadian novice singles title in 1996, and was third in Juniors in 2000, the same year he and Jennifer Dubois were junior pairs silver medalists.

"It was always understood Sean would be a pairs skater," said Paul Wirtz, who is not only the pair's coach, but also Sean's uncle.

Putnam and Wirtz formed their team in June 2002, after her partnership with Batka broke up. While they still had lots of work to do on their connecting steps and maneuvers, they immediately had what skaters call the "wow" factor. In their first major competition together, they were fifth after the short program at Canadian Nationals, but finished second in the freeskate to capture the bronze medal. They were placed on the Grand Prix circuit for 2002–03, giving Canada more depth than the country had anticipated after Salé and Pelletier turned pro.

"We came a long way in our first year," Putnam said. Skating insiders figure they'll be going a lot further.

Born: November 28, 1984, Toronto,Ontario;
October 31, 1979, Marathon, Ontario

Hometowns: Toronto, Marathon

Training Site: Toronto

Coach: Paul Wirtz

Choreographer: Steven Belanger

RESULTS

2003: 9th Four Continents
3rd Canadian Nationals

- The Wirtzes are among Canada's pre-eminent skating families. Sean's uncles Paul and Kris, both of whom now help coach Elizabeth and Sean, were successful competitors. Kris, who competed 19 years at Nationals, won the Canadian pairs title twice with his wife, Kristy.

- Both Sean and Elizabeth will continue singles skating in order to improve their partnership. "Doing jumps under pressure in singles really helps me in pairs," Elizabeth says.

Canadians | Saskatoon | January 2003

Dorota Zagorska & Mariusz Siudek

To understand just how committed Dorota Zagorska and Mariusz Siudek are to their pairs partnership, it is necessary to know something about May 13, 2000. It's their wedding day.

"It was our only day off from training," Zagorska explains. "We were back on the ice the next day."

Zagorska and Siudek don't like to skip practice, even for a wedding, because ice time has been at a premium during their careers. They used to spend three weeks of every summer at a rink in Chicago because no arena in Poland had summer ice.

"But now, we train only in Oswiecim; our rink is good there," Siudek says proudly. Zagorska also competed in singles, while Siudek skated internationally with a few other partners.

The couple are the only Polish pairs team to win a medal at the World Championships – a bronze at Helsinki in 1999. Their performance at 2001 Worlds would have been medal-caliber in almost any other year, but 2001 was a one-of-a-kind championship. The crowd gave the entertaining Polish pair a rousing standing ovation, but they finished sixth.

They want their international success to inspire younger Polish skaters. They plan to open a skating school in Oswiecim, based on the Russian model.

"There are only eight ice rinks working for 10 months a year in Poland," Siudek says. "There are more than that in Vancouver alone.

"When we started, there was just a wish that we wanted to try skating. There were no such things as role models."

There are now.

• Mariusz proposed to Dorota at the closing banquet of 2000 Worlds, with dozens of other skaters watching!

Worlds | Washington | March 2003 ◉

Born: September 9, 1975, Krakow, Poland; April 29, 1972, Oswiecim

Hometowns: Krakow, Oswiecim

Training Site: Oswiecim

Coaches: Richard Gauthier, Iwona Mydiarz-Chruscinska

Choreographers: Frantisek Blatak, Vladimir Chernysov

RESULTS

2001: 6th Worlds
4th Grand Prix Final
4th Cup of Russia
3rd NHK
2nd Goodwill Games

2002: 7th Olympics
6th Worlds
4th Europeans
3rd Bofrost Cup
4th Cup of Russia
2nd NHK

2003: 7th Worlds
5th Grand Prix Final
4th Europeans

Worlds | Vancouver | March 2001

Yuko Kawaguchi & Alexander Markuntsov

You have to give Yuko Kawaguchi full marks for perseverance. Her coach certainly does. Kawaguchi, who was skating singles at the time, fell in love with Elena Berezhnaya's pairs skating during the 1998 Olympics and somehow obtained the fax number of Berezhnaya's coach, Tamara Moskvina. She asked Moskvina if she would train her too. "She was very persistent," Moskvina recalls.

Eventually, Kawaguchi moved from her home in Chiba, Japan, to Moskvina's new training center in Hackensack, New Jersey, and also decided she wanted to switch from singles to pairs. But Moskvina had a policy of coaching only three pairs at a time, and she already had a full slate.

When Artur Dmitriev and Oksana Kazakova turned pro in 1999, there was room for another pair, and Moskvina's husband, Igor Moskvin, had a Russian skater who was looking for a new partner. Alexander (Sasha) Markuntsov and Valentina Raskazova had represented Russia internationally with some degree of success, but she had retired and gone back to school. So the Japanese singles skater and the Russian pairs skater got together at an American rink, and decided to compete for Japan.

Moskvina developed the partnership around the pair's jumping ability and the flexibility Kawaguchi had developed as a young ballerina. They demonstrate some unusual lifts, a Moskvina coaching trademark, and also do a triple-double jump combination. They made their international debut on the 2000 Junior Grand Prix series and finished second at Junior Worlds in 2001, the same year they won the Japanese junior title.

They won Senior Nationals in 2002 and were 13th at Worlds, but because Markuntsov is not a Japanese citizen, they could not compete at the Olympics. The pair split up for three months in 2002. But after looking for new partners they decided they were best for each other. They are working on a throw quadruple Lutz, which would move them quickly up the ranks. And if Markuntsov is as persistent as Kawaguchi has been, they'll have the quad in no time.

Born: November 20, 1981, Aichi, Japan; February 21, 1982, St. Petersburg, Russia

Hometowns: Aichi, St. Petersburg

Training Site: Hackensack, New Jersey

Coaches: Igor Moskvin, Tamara Moskvina

Choreographers: Tatiana Druchinina, Igor Bobrin, Tamara Moskvina

RESULTS

2001: 15th Worlds
8th Four Continents
2nd World Juniors
6th Skate America
6th Lalique Trophy

2002: 13th Worlds
7th Four Continents
1st Japanese Nationals
5th Skate America
5th NHK

2003: 14th Worlds
7th Four Continents
1st Japanese Nationals

Skate America | Spokane | October 2002

• Sasha and Yuko's silver medal at the Junior Worlds was the first major international medal won by a pairs team representing Japan.

Rena Inoue & John Baldwin

There is experience, and then there is real experience. Rena Inoue and John Baldwin Jr. may be a relatively new pairs team, but they're veterans of the skating world.

Inoue and Baldwin were raised half a world apart, but they both began skating because they had to. When Inoue was four years old, a doctor in her native Japan suggested that she take up swimming and figure skating to combat her asthma. She stayed with skating and succeeded in two disciplines. In the 1992 Olympics, when she was 15, Inoue finished 14th in pairs with Tomoaki Koyama; and in the 1994 Games, she was 18th in singles.

Baldwin, meanwhile, grew up in Dallas – and was skating almost as soon as he could walk because his parents, Donna and John Sr., ran the only all-season rink in the city.

In 1986, at the age of 12, Baldwin began his long string of appearances at the U.S. Nationals. As a singles skater, he won the bronze medal at the 1990 World Junior Championships and the U.S. Juniors title in 1991. But as quads became increasingly necessary for success in singles, Baldwin began to consider a second career in pairs. He was looking for someone with the jumping ability of a singles skater and the skating experience that could match his. Inoue fit the bill, and they teamed up in 2000. Eventually, they became an off-ice couple as well.

Inoue should have her U.S. citizenship in plenty of time for the 2006 Olympics, when she and Baldwin hope

Born: October 17, 1976, Nishinomiya, Japan; October 18, 1973, Dallas

Hometown: Santa Monica, California

Training Site: Aliso Viejo, California

Coach: Jill Watson

Choreographer: Burt Lancon

RESULTS

2001: 11th U.S. Nationals

2002: 7th Four Continents
4th U.S. Nationals
5th Bofrost Cup
5th Cup of Russia

2003: 10th Worlds
3rd U.S. Nationals

Worlds | Washington | March 2003

Worlds | Washington | March 2003

- Rena attended medical school in Los Angeles, but has put her studies on hold to concentrate on skating.

- In 2003 John made his 14th straight appearance at Nationals, and his 16th in 17 years.

to become the first U.S. pair to medal since 1988. That year the bronze was won by Americans Peter Oppegard and Jill Watson, who is now the coach of Inoue and Baldwin.

THE
DANCE
TEAMS

Shae-Lynn Bourne and Victor Kraatz

Irina Lobacheva and Ilia Averbukh

Albena Denkova and Maxim Staviyski

Galit Chait and Sergei Sakhnovski

Elena Grushina and Ruslan Goncharov

Naomi Lang and Peter Tchernyshev

Tanith Belbin and Benjamin Agosto

Marie-France Dubreuil and Patrice Lauzon

Tatiana Navka and Roman Kostomarov

Isabelle Delobel and Olivier Schoenfelder

Kati Winkler and Rene Lohse

Megan Wing and Aaron Lowe

Federica Faiella and Massimo Scali

If change is healthy, then ice dancing must finally be getting well. Since it became an Olympic event in 1976, ice dancing has been plagued by severe judging controversies, rigid rankings and monopolization by one country. Still, it is almost always the first skating event sold out at the Olympic Games. And the 2003 World Championships graphically illustrated that a new era was dawning for a skating division that handles

change the way water handles oil. For the first time, a couple from North America stood on top of the podium.

The gold medal won by Canada's Shae-Lynn Bourne and Victor Kraatz culminated a brilliant career that was not rewarded nearly often enough by dance's judging panels. It also gave hope to every other skating nation, particularly those that don't compete at Europeans, that their dancers may some day have a real chance instead of just a theoretical one. In an emotional finale to their amateur careers,

Bourne and Kraatz defeated defending champions Irina Lobacheva and Ilia Averbukh of Russia, the country that has always wielded the power in ice dancing.

The Russians intimated that the North American site of the Worlds (Washington, D.C.) had something to do with the final result. That might have been dreadfully poor sportsmanship, but it accidentally referred to another impressive change in ice dancing's most rigid division. The heart of ice dancing is now in the United States of America, which has never won a world title.

That said, the blood of that heart is still mostly Russian. Of the top eight couples at 2003 Worlds, all but one – Bulgaria's Albena Denkova and Maxim Staviyski – are based at American training sites. That's mainly because, after the Russian economy sagged with the dissolution of the Soviet Union, Russia's three leading dance coaches (Tatiana Tarasova, Natalia Linichuk and Natalia Dubova) came to the United States. A younger generation of rising Russian-trained coaching stars – such as Igor Shpilband, Alexander Zhulin and Evgeny Platov – have also established teaching careers in America. And six of the top eight couples at 2003 Worlds had at least one team member who was born and trained in Russia, where respect for ice dancing runs deep.

From 1969 to 1999, couples from Russia or the old Soviet Union won 25 of 31 world titles and six of seven Olympic golds. But that tight grip has been loosening over

recent years. Marina Anissina and Gwendal Peizerat of France won Worlds in 2000 and Olympics in 2002, while Barbara Fusar-Poli and Maurizio Margaglio gave Italy its first ice dancing World Championship in 2001. At 2000 Worlds, Russia did not win an ice dance medal for the first time in 36 years. And in 2003, Tanith Belbin and Benjamin Agosto combined with Naomi Lang and Peter Tchernyshev to give the United States two couples in the top 10 for the first time in 13 years.

To many fans, dancing is the most entertaining discipline in skating. It is certainly the most theatrical. Because ice dancers are freed from the burden of landing difficult individual jumps or dangerous pairs throws, there is more room for creativity and expression. The accent is on rhythm, translating precise dance-floor steps to the faster medium of ice, and showcasing two people united in their interpretation of music.

Ice dancing differs from pairs and singles skating in a

number of ways. The costumes are more elaborate, and the storytelling in the programs is more complex. With only a few brief exceptions, the partners must maintain contact with each other throughout the dance, and one foot of each skater must be on the ice. There are no jumps, which separates the way dancers practice from the way other skaters do. As a result, ice dancers tend to be of different body shapes – taller and leaner, generally – and athletic temperaments than singles skaters.

Ice dance is also the only discipline that has retained a "compulsory" segment. Singles skating got rid of compulsory figures in 1990, and pairs never had them. But ice dancers still must perform two compulsory dances – the same for all teams – each worth 10 percent of the final result. The original dance is worth 30 percent and must be skated to a certain rhythm (tango, polka, blues, etc.), but the skaters design their own programs. The freedance, worth 50 percent, can be skated to any accompaniment, including music with vocals, and allows the couples to unleash the full force of their speed and creativity.

After serious complaints about judging at the 1998 Winter Olympics, the rules of ice dancing became more formalized. Judging panels are chosen only at the last minute. Falls and stumbles are now penalized, there are limits on the number of separations and small lifts in a freedance, and certain standard elements are required.

While champions may change more regularly, there is still suspicion of the results – many skaters and coaches signed a petition of protest at Worlds – and little movement once a competition starts. At 2003 Worlds, the final order from No. 3 to No. 16 was the same as it had been after the original dance. But, as Victor Kraatz said in the first edition of *Figure Skating Now,* although much more reform is still

required, ice dancers have increasing evidence that if they skate well, they will be rewarded. He and Shae-Lynn Bourne are the brightest examples of that.

Shae-Lynn Bourne & Victor Kraatz

When their long, and often painful, journey to the top of the world was finally over, Victor Kraatz lay down on the ice. Thousands of fans at the 2003 World Championships in Washington were on their feet voicing their approval, his partner of 12 years was bending over and hugging him, and still Kraatz didn't move. "I was just savoring the moment," said Kraatz after he and Shae-Lynn Bourne had become the first ice dancers representing a North American country ever to win the World Championship. "I was reflecting over all the years of being so close and not winning a medal at the Olympics, and so close and not getting the gold last year. I'm just so very happy."

And so was an entire country. For 12 years, Canadians had been impressed as Bourne and Kraatz injected athleticism and speed into a discipline that critics were beginning to call cheap theatre. They were awed as Bourne and Kraatz invented "hydroblading," the low-to-the-ice, gravity-defying technique that was the inspiration for many of today's revolutionary ice dancing moves. Canadians had been hopeful as their popular champions quickly moved up the rigid hierarchy of world ice dance, then stalled at third place – held back, most felt, by judging irregularities. And a whole country felt for them when injuries ruined the 1999–2000 season and threatened to disrupt the 2002–03 season, which the couple had already announced would be their last in amateur ranks.

And what a finale it was. Bourne and Kraatz, who had won two Grand Prix Finals, missed the entire Grand Prix season in 2002 because of Bourne's ankle injury. They returned in time to bid farewell to Canada, with their 10th national title, and were given a string of nine perfect 6.0s for presentation. Bourne and Kraatz had won a world silver

- In 1992 Bourne and Kraatz captured their first important title, the Canadian Junior Nationals. But because of a skull fracture, Bourne had to wear a helmet during practices.

- Victor speaks four languages: English, Italian, German and French.

Worlds | Washington | March 2003

Olympics | Salt Lake City | February 2002

Born: January 24, 1976, Chatham, Ontario; April 7, 1971, Berlin

Hometowns: Chatham, Vancouver, B.C.

Training Site: Newington, Connecticut

Coach: Nikolai Morozov

Choreographer: Nikolai Morozov

RESULTS

1998: 4th Olympics
3rd Worlds
2nd Grand Prix Final
1st Skate Canada
1st Canadian Nationals

1999: 3rd Worlds
1st Four Continents
1st Sparkassen Cup
2nd Cup of Russia
1st Canadian Nationals

2000: 5th Grand Prix Final
3rd Sparkassen Cup
3rd Skate America

2001: 4th Worlds
1st Four Continents
1st Canadian Nationals

2002: 4th Olympics
2nd Worlds
1st Grand Prix Final
1st Canadian Nationals

2003: 1st Worlds
1st Four Continents
1st Canadian Nationals

Worlds | Washington | March 2003

Worlds | Washington | March 2003

medal in 2002, and were hopeful that the "anonymous" judging system, which was a bridge between the old system and a radical new proposal set to arrive in two years, would help them overcome past judging biases. And it did.

Bourne and Kraatz had helped change the way ice dancing, and skating in general, are judged. New, more definitive rules for marking were introduced after the 1998 Olympics when they did not win a medal despite their brilliant "Riverdance" freeskate, the most memorable ice dance program since France's Duchesnays retired in 1992.

The partnership almost didn't happen. In April 1991, Kraatz conducted a cross-country search for a new partner and test-skated with more than a dozen young women without success. After another failed session in Montreal, he was about to leave the rink when the arena manager suggested he take a spin with a dynamic 16-year-old who was new to ice dancing.

"Five minutes later, Shae-Lynn and I decided to try it for one week, and then I asked her to skate with me," Kraatz recalls. "It's still the best decision I ever made."

It was a great match. They had similar lines, both are very athletic and fast on their feet and they each have what skaters refer to as "soft knees," which allow for smooth, deep strokes. And each had the burning will to achieve.

Bourne was raised in a sports-minded family in the

western Ontario town of Chatham, and was originally a pairs skater but loved the rhythm and speed of ice dancing. Kraatz, born in West Berlin, was raised in an Italian-speaking region in Switzerland. His first love was skiing, but he kept injuring himself. So when he was 10 his mother suggested he take skating lessons. He eventually won the Swiss junior ice dance championships before his family moved to Canada in 1987.

Once Bourne and Kraatz found each other, their rise was spectacular. They finished 14th in their world debut in 1993, 10th in the Olympics and sixth at Worlds in Edmonton, the first podium placing by a North American dance team since Tracy Wilson and Rob McCall in 1988. They also won bronze each of the next three years, the Grand Prix Final in 1997, and 25 international medals, spectacular achievements in a discipline absolutely dominated since its inception by Europeans.

Along the way, Bourne and Kraatz have changed coaches and training sites several times. After the disappointment of the 1998 Olympics and declining results in 1999–2000, Kraatz considered retiring from the sport. The couple decided to renew their commitment to skating, but also decided they needed some kind of fresh start. So they switched from Natalia Dubova, whom they highly respected, to new coach Tatiana Tarasova, in Newington, Connecticut.

Champion Series Final | Hamilton | December 1997

Bourne and Kraatz returned to competition for the 2000–01 season, after her second knee surgery in two years. They were better trained, with more of the emotion that has characterized European dancers. But they had not abandoned their quick footwork, hydro-blading and enthusiasm. Despite missing the previous Worlds, they finished fourth in 2001, missing the podium by one judge. They won the Grand Prix Final the next season, but narrowly missed the podium at the 2002 Olympics, amid charges that the results were predetermined. A month later, they won silver at Worlds, the highest Canadian finish in 38 years. But in the middle of their final season, Tarasova changed rinks and announced she wasn't coaching the Canadians any more. Co-coach and choreographer Nikolai Morozov took over.

It was one of Tarasova's rare poor decisions. Just a few months later, Bourne and Kraatz edged defending champions Irina Lobacheva and Ilia Averbukh to win the World Championship most people thought should have been theirs before then. But better late than never. As Kraatz lay on the ice at the 2003 Worlds in Washington, after their brilliant freeskate (which called for world peace) had ended in triumph, Bourne leaned over and whispered something to him. "We've changed and grown together," she said of their conversation. "I said, 'Thank you.'" And so did a whole country.

Worlds | Vancouver | March 2001

Irina Lobacheva & Ilia Averbukh

In every sport with a podium, the most detested finish is **fourth place**. It's like pressing your nose against the window of the candy store.

Irina Lobacheva and her husband, Ilia Averbukh, knew that feeling too well. They finished fourth in three straight World Championships – from 1998 through 2000 – and also in two European Championships. And when they fell just short of the podium in 2000, it marked the first time that Russia had not won at least one ice dancing medal at Worlds since 1965.

But Lobacheva and Averbukh began a new Russian streak in 2001, finishing third in the world with their swirling interpretation of Bach's music. It capped a satisfying season in which they also won bronze at Europeans, took silvers at two Grand Prix events and at the Grand Prix Final, and won their second successive National Championship.

"If you don't win a medal, then the whole season doesn't feel right," Averbukh said. If so, then their seasons have certainly felt right since then. After their breakthrough year in 2000–01, Lobacheva and Averbukh established themselves as the team to beat in ice dancing, although, like most things in their long career, that status did not come easily.

Six months after their first world medal, the couple won the Goodwill Games in Brisbane, Australia. Then Lobacheva suffered an injury to her left knee during a practice. In the all-important run-up to the Olympics, Lobacheva and Averbukh were forced to take a month away from training. They had to skip all their assignments on the Grand Prix circuit, which can be severely damaging in ice dancing, a discipline in which momentum has a great deal to do with how the judges regard couples. She should have had surgery, but Lobacheva decided it was too important a year to miss. So she returned to the ice, skating in pain at every session.

The couple made a stunning return by finishing third at Europeans. "We had more power after that and our skating

Born: February 18, 1973, Ivanteeka, Russia
December 18, 1973, Moscow

Hometown: Moscow

Training Site: Newark, Delaware

Coaches: Natalia Linichuk, Gennadi Karponosov

Choreographer: Natalia Linichuk

RESULTS

2000: 4th Worlds
4th Europeans

2001: 3rd Worlds
3rd Europeans
2nd Grand Prix Final

2002: 2nd Olympics
1st Worlds
1st Grand Prix Final
3rd Europeans
1st Cup of Russia
1st NHK

2003: 2nd Words
1st Grand Prix Final
1st Europeans

Olympics | Nagano | February 1998

• Both Irina and Ilia began as singles skaters. Ilia preferred soccer and hockey, but stayed in skating and switched to ice dancing when he was 12.

got stronger," Lobacheva said. That was an understatement, as he and his wife went on to win a silver medal at the Olympics. Then, with Olympic champions Marina Anissina

Worlds | Washington | March 2003

and Gwendal Peizerat graduating to the pros, Lobacheva and Averbukh returned Russia to the top of the dance podium for the first time in three years, ending the ice dancing superpower's longest gold-medal drought since 1984. "It was a long trip, but we are very happy now because we won the gold," Averbukh said of their tearful triumph. "Eight years for this medal."

The couple made their Worlds debut in 1994, finishing 13th. That same year they got married, culminating a love story that began when Averbukh was skating with Marina Anissina, with whom he had won Junior Worlds in 1990 and 1992. But Averbukh had noticed – and fallen in love with – Lobacheva, who also skated in their training group

in Moscow. So he broke up his partnership with Anissina and joined with Lobacheva in 1992. (Ironically, it was Anissina and her new partner who beat them for the Olympic gold almost exactly a decade later.)

As the Russian economy failed, Lobacheva recalls, the newly married couple "were having trouble finding training time and enough to eat." And their difficulties were reflected in their world results. After dropping to 15th in 1995, they left for Delaware to join coach Natalia Linichuk, who had preceded them to the United States. It was exactly what the couple needed. They jumped nine places to finish sixth at 1995 Worlds and began their long final push toward the top of the podium.

Worlds | Washington | March 2003

Worlds | Washington | March 2003

Worlds | Washington | March 2003

They have always said that they would return to Russia as soon as they retired. Lobacheva wants to open a fitness club, and Averbukh hopes to work as a TV journalist. Originally, they thought their 2001–02 season would be their final one in eligible ranks, but they put their retirement off for a year, probably two, after they won Worlds.

Feeling the confidence of champions, they had an outstanding season in 2002–03 and were undefeated in big events until they were edged for the gold medal at Worlds by Shae-Lynn Bourne and Victor Kraatz.

Albena Denkova & Maxim Staviyski

For a few years, if it weren't for bad luck, they would have had no luck at all. But when they climbed onto the podium to receive their bronze medals at the 2003 World Championships, Albena Denkova and Maxim Staviyski were thinking about the present and future, not the past.

Their medal was the first-ever at the World Championships for Bulgaria. And the couple's recent surge in the rankings has made figure skating what Denkova calls "the most popular winter sport in our country." Just two years earlier, Denkova and Staviyski had become the first Bulgarian couple to crack the top 10, when they finished 10th at Worlds in Vancouver. But only a few months before that, it appeared that they would never skate as a couple again.

The 2000s began horribly for Denkova and Staviyski, when he came down with a heavy case of pneumonia for three weeks and they had to withdraw from Europeans. After he recovered in time to enter 2000 Worlds at Nice, the couple was headed for a top-10 finish when Denkova collided with U.S. dancer Peter Tchernyshev at a practice on the morning of the freedance. It was a gruesome scene. Tchernyshev's blade severed two tendons and a muscle in Denkova's lower leg, and she was rushed to a hospital where she underwent surgery and spent a week in recovery.

She was flown home to Bulgaria, and she had to spend six weeks in bed and another two months with her leg in a hard cast. For many months, whenever she skated the leg would balloon horribly. (She still feels pain in the old injury when the weather changes.) Then, when Denkova innocently inquired whether the United States Figure Skating Association had insurance that might cover the accident, rumors began circulating in the skating community that she was going

Born: December 3, 1974, Sofia, Bulgaria;
November 16, 1977, Rostov-na-Don, Russia

Hometown: Odintsovo, Russia/Sofia

Coach: Alexei Gorshkov

Choreographer: Sergei Petukhov

RESULTS

1999: 11th Worlds
9th Europeans
3rd Sparkassen Cup
6th NHK

2000: 1st Finlandia Trophy

2001: 8th Europeans
10th Worlds
4th Lalique Trophy
3rd NHK

2002: 7th Olympics
5th Worlds
6th Europeans
1st Bofrost Cup
3rd Cup of Russia
4th Skate Canada

2003: 3rd Worlds
2nd Europeans
3rd Grand Prix Final

• Albena has a university degree in economics, but she may become a clothing designer.

• Maxim has a degree from a sports institute and may go into coaching in Bulgaria, where skating has become more popular.

Worlds | Washington | March 2003

"We are a small federation with no traditions in figure skating – particularly in ice dancing – so it is very difficult for us," Denkova explains. "If we don't do something different, nobody will see us; nobody will notice us."

Judges saw and judges noticed. After their horrible accident, Denkova and Staviyski made it back into competition late in the fall of 2000 – although an invitation to Skate America was reportedly withdrawn – and the couple finished eighth at Europeans and 10th at 2001 Worlds. In 2002, they were seventh at Olympics and fifth at Worlds in Nagano, and were elated at their progress. "Four years ago we were in this same place, Nagano, and finished 18th at Olympics," Denkova said. "And now just four years later we are fifth. We think that's a big improvement."

A more important improvement was on the horizon. After they won their first Grand Prix event (Bofrost Cup) in the fall of 2002, they took a silver at Europeans and won their country's first skating medal at Worlds.

Standing on the podium together was not something they could have imagined when they began their careers in separate countries. Denkova started out as a gymnast, as so many young Bulgarian girls do. But with the depth of that sport in her country, she realized she would have

Worlds | Washington | March 2003

to sue the association. But she says that was never her intention.

The couple moved from Sofia in Bulgaria to Odintsovo, near Moscow, in September 2000, so they could train daily with their choreographer, Sergei Petukhov, who works with them on their innovative and attention-getting maneuvers.

Worlds | Washington | March 2003

trouble reaching the top. So, at the age of nine, she switched to figure skating – "but I could not jump" – and took up ice dancing when she was 12.

She was partnered with Hristo Nikolov, and they skated together until 1995. He was not as ambitious as she was, and he eventually retired from the sport. That left her without a partner, and after she searched Russia, Canada, the United States and France for a proper match, she became disillusioned. "At the end of the year, I said, 'I'm quitting. There's no other way.'" She went without a partner for a year, but a chance conversation between Russian and Bulgarian officials at 1996 Worlds resulted in a tryout with Staviyski, who was three years younger and also looking for a new start.

Staviyski had been a singles skater. At the age of 12 he broke his leg. His jumping power diminished, so he switched to ice dancing. He was teamed with Anastasia

Belova, but when he became too old for Juniors, she wanted to remain in junior skating and the partnership dissolved. So, Denkova and Staviyski auditioned together in Moscow.

"Our first moments together were not great," Staviyski recalls. "She was a bit scared of Moscow, and I was a bit crazy." But the couple kept at it, which became their trademark trait. He applied for Bulgarian citizenship, and the new team spent good portions of the year training on their own in Sofia, traveling to Moscow occasionally to get input from coach Alexei Gorshkov.

"Maxim was a much better skater than I was, and I had to improve every year in order to get closer to his abilities," Denkova explains. As she did that, the couple began slowly climbing the ranks. And by 2003, they had got rid of their bad luck and replaced it with something else: Bulgaria's first World Championship medal.

Galit Chait & Sergei Sakhnovski

It took Galit Chait and Sergei Sakhnovski many years to become an overnight success. Most of the skating community began to take notice of Israel's ice dancers only in 2000 – when they rocketed to fifth place at Worlds, after languishing in 13th the previous season. And they really paid attention when Chait and Sakhnovski won Israel's first-ever World Championship medal with a bronze at the 2002 Worlds in Nagano. But these weren't newcomers to the sport. They had spent four years together in the lower reaches of the world ice dance rankings, and well before that had skated internationally with other partners.

Chait, born in Israel but raised in the United States, had finished 28th at 1994 Worlds with Maxim Savostianov. Moscow-born Sakhnovski, who started as a singles skater, won the World Junior Championship with Ekaterina Svirina for Russia in 1993.

They began their partnership in 1995 and have skated for a bevy of different coaches, each of whom added key building blocks to their technique and style. They trained with Natalia Linichuk, then Tatiana Tarasova before moving to a third Russian legend, Natalia Dubova in 2001. Dubova helped them to their World bronze before the couple moved again in the summer of 2002 to two-time Olympic champion Evgeny Platov. Platov is retooling their basic technique, a work-in-progress that might help explain their drop to sixth place at 2003 Worlds.

The highlight of their career to date was their medal at 2002 Worlds, but it was also a low point. In the wake of years of judging scandals, several skaters and coaches signed a petition protesting the bronze medal results. Chait and Sakhnovski were stung by the reaction, because many of their longtime friends were involved.

But they have vowed to ignore their pain and concentrate on giving Israel its first Olympic skating medal at the 2006 Games. "We don't have time to think about what people are saying or writing about us," Chait says.

Worlds | Washington | March 2003

Born: January 29, 1975, Kfar-Saba, Israel; May 15, 1975, Moscow

Hometowns: Metulla, Israel; Moscow

Training Site: Freehold, New Jersey

Coach: Evgeny Platov

Choreographer: Ivan Fadeev

RESULTS

2000: 5th Worlds
6th Europeans
2nd Skate Canada
3rd Cup of Russia
4th Skate America

2001: 6th Worlds
5th Grand Prix Final
5th Europeans
2nd Cup of Russia
2nd Skate America

2002: 6th Olympics
3rd Worlds
5th Europeans
2nd Bofrost Cup
4th Skate America
3rd NHK

2003: 6th Worlds
6th Europeans
5th Grand Prix Final

Skate Canada | Mississauga | November 2000

- Israel, which had no Olympic skaters before 1994, had five in the 2002 Games, led by Galit and Sergei.

- Galit and Sergei finished 23rd, 18th, 14th and 13th at Worlds before rocketing to 5th in 2000.

Elena Grushina & Ruslan Goncharov

Elena Grushina and Ruslan Goncharov would rather **dance than jump.** So it's a good thing they each decided to give up singles skating.

When Grushina started skating at the age of four, and Goncharov started at the age of six, neither chose ice dancing. Eventually Goncharov realized he would grow to be too tall (he's 6'1") to be an effective singles skater, while Grushina came to see that skating in a couple would be more interesting than training on her own. Since each had studied ballet from a young age, ice dancing seemed an obvious destination.

They were in the same training group in their hometown of Odessa, Ukraine, but coaches there decided that Grushina should skate with Mikhail Tashliski and Goncharov should team with Eleonora Grinsaya. But within two years both partnerships were over. It seemed natural that the two remaining partners should join forces – so natural that they became a couple away from the rink as well. They married in 1995.

Sometimes the hardest part of ice dancing is the waiting. Irina Romanova and Igor Yaroshenko were dominating Ukrainian ice dancing, so it took time for Grushina and Goncharov to make their mark. Grushina and Goncharov made their world debut in 1994 and finished 18th. In the brief absence of Romanova and Yaroshenko, they won their first national title in 1995. But they could not win another until 1999.

They hovered in the middle of the world ice dance pack for several years, climbing as high as 13th at 1998 Worlds. By then they had moved to Newark, Delaware, to train with Natalia Linichuk and Gennadi Karponosov, because their rink in Odessa had closed down.

In the United States, they had better practice time and access to clearly recorded music, something they didn't have in Ukraine, and they climbed into the top 10. After six years with Linichuk, they moved to Tatiana Tarasova's camp in 2002, and had their best season ever. They won all three of their Grand Prix events, and had their highest finishes at Europeans (4th) and Worlds (5th).

Born: January 8, 1975, Odessa, Ukraine; January 20, 1973, Odessa

Hometown: Odessa

Training Site: Wethersfield, Connecticut

Coach: Tatiana Tarasova

Choreographers: Tatiana Tarasova, Maia Usova

RESULTS

2000: 7th Worlds
8th Europeans
4th Skate Canada
4th NHK

2001: 8th Worlds
7th Europeans
3rd Cup of Russia
5th NHK

2002: 9th Olympics
6th Worlds
8th Europeans
1st Skate America
1st Skate Canada
1st Lalique Trophy

2003: 5th Worlds
4th Europeans
4th Grand Prix Final

• Elena's hobbies are reading and billiards. Ruslan prefers tennis and fishing.

⬆ Worlds | Washington | March 2003

⬅ Worlds | Washington | March 2003

Naomi Lang & Peter Tchernyshev

Peter Tchernyshev insists that he feels "more like I am just a citizen of planet Earth than I am a Russian or an American." On January 29, 2001, at a ceremony in Detroit, Tchernyshev became an American citizen. At his side was Naomi Lang, with whom he had already won three consecutive American ice dancing championships.

Tchernyshev was born in Russia and skated singles until he was 18, when injuries began impeding his jumps. So he concentrated on ice dancing. In 1992 he moved to the United States, and at the 1996 U.S. Nationals he noticed a 15-year-old junior dancer who was "very expressive." He suggested they form a partnership. Naomi Lang agreed.

Lang was a ballet dancer talented enough to perform with the Grand Rapids Ballet Company. She was inspired to start skating as an eight-year-old after seeing the Ice Capades. She and her mother sewed Naomi's costumes themselves at the kitchen table.

Lang is a natural, passionate dancer, but because Tchernyshev is eight years older and was more experienced, at the beginning it was an unbalanced partnership. But gradually Lang matured, and early in 2001 Tchernyshev said, "She is doing some things better than me."

They are blessed with attractive lines and enviable technique, and have firmly established themselves among the world's top 10. But they want to push into the final flight. When they moved from Michigan to New Jersey in 2000 to work with former world champion Sasha Zhulin, he injected a spark of fresh enthusiasm into their work. Then they switched to Tatiana Tarasova, but remained with Nikolai Morozov when Tarasova changed sites in late 2002. Lang's ankle injury forced them out of the 2002–03 fall competition. But with only minimal training they won their fifth straight U.S. title and earned their fifth top-10 finish at Worlds.

Born: December 18, 1978, Arcata, California;
February 6, 1971, St. Petersburg, Russia

Hometowns: Allegan, Michigan; St. Petersburg

Training Site: Newington, Connecticut

Coach: Nikolai Morozov

Choreographer: Nikolai Morozov

RESULTS

1999: 10th Worlds
3rd Four Continents
3rd Skate America
5th Lalique Trophy

2000: 8th Worlds
1st Four Continents
1st U.S. Nationals
5th Skate America
4th Lalique Trophy

2001: 9th Worlds
2nd Four Continents

2002: 11th Olympics
9th Worlds
1st Four Continents

2003: 8th Worlds
3rd Four Continents

Four Continents | Salt Lake City | February 2001

- Naomi is a member of the west coast Native American Karuk tribe. She wants to be a role model for Native American children.

- Peter's grandfather, also named Peter, was men's skating champion of Russia from 1936 to 1939.

Tanith Belbin & Benjamin Agosto

What goes around comes around, but not necessarily in the same form.

In March of 2001, Tanith Belbin returned to Vancouver's GM Place, four years after she'd first competed in the massive arena. At the 1997 Canadian Championships, Belbin was a 12-year-old pairs skater living in a Montreal suburb. She and partner Benjamin Barrucco won a silver medal in novice pairs.

At the 2001 World Championships, Belbin was a 16-year-old ice dancer, living in a Detroit suburb and skating for the United States. She and another Benjamin – 19-year-old Benjamin Agosto – finished 17th in their world debut.

"I spent a year in Canada looking for an ice dancing partner, but couldn't find one," Belbin says of her cross-border alliance.

Agosto's coaches, Igor Shpilband and Elizabeth Coates, ran into Belbin's coach, Paul Wirtz, at the Nagano Olympics. As a result, Belbin moved to Agosto's training base in Detroit, and the international alliance was forged.

"It's something you see very often in ice dancing," Agosto says. "You have to look everywhere for the best partner, and I'm just thankful for this."

The couple has had a relatively quick rise through ice dancing's rigid hierarchy. They won the U.S. junior title on their first attempt in 2000, then won silver at Senior Nationals the next two years. In 2003 they were leading after the original dance, but a late slip relegated them to second again. But when they won silver at Four Continents, it was the first time in seven attempts they had beaten U.S. champions Naomi Lang and Peter Tchernyshev. They did it again when they leapt to a stunning seventh place at Worlds.

They were ineligible for the 2002 Olympics, but hope to have Belbin's U.S. citizenship in time for 2006.

"That's an intricate process," Belbin says. "So we're just going to keep the focus on our skating."

Belbin and her mother, Michelle, a skating coach and costume designer, moved to Michigan in 1998. A year later, her father, Charles, obtained a transfer, so he and son Lucas could join the rest of the family.

Born: July 11, 1984, Kingston, Ontario; January 15, 1982, Chicago

Hometowns: Montreal, Quebec; Beverly Hills, Illinois

Training Site: Bloomfield Hills, Michigan

Coaches: Igor Shpilband, Marina Zoueva

Choreographer: Igor Shpilband

Worlds | Washington
March 2003

RESULTS

2001: 17th Worlds
1st Junior Grand Prix Final
6th Lalique Trophy

2002: 13th Worlds
2nd Four Continents
3rd Skate America
3rd Lalique Trophy

2003: 7th Worlds
2nd Four Continents

"It was a great sacrifice for everyone," Belbin says. "It shows what kind of support we have."

• Tanith and Benjamin were still juniors when they competed at 2001 Worlds.

Skate America | Spokane | October 2002

Marie-France Dubreuil & Patrice Lauzon

Marie-France Dubreuil and Patrice Lauzon had fallen in love, but they were the last to know.

"Everybody saw it except us; it took us some time to recognize it," Dubreuil recalls with a smile. "But you can only fight your feelings for a while."

The couple stopped fighting their feelings a year after they became an ice dancing team in 1995. Even that partnership took them some time to figure out. They had been good friends and had trained at the same Montreal rink for years, with different partners. Dubreuil won a Junior world bronze medal with Bruno Yvars, while Lauzon was fourth at World Juniors with Chantal Lefebvre.

"We were all at Patrice's cottage, just friends having fun," Dubreuil says. "Patrice was taking a year off and I had quit my partnership. I said, 'Maybe we should try.' And it worked."

Right away. They finished a surprising fourth in their first Nationals. But then they hit a plateau, stalling in fourth place for three more years. They became discouraged and considered retiring, but decided to give it until the end of the 1999–2000 season.

And what a season it was. With Shae-Lynn Bourne and Victor Kraatz sidelined by injury, Dubreuil and Lauzon won the Canadian championship in January 2000, then took a silver medal at Four Continents. Impressed by their combination of North American and European styles (they spent three weeks each year training in Lyon, France), judges placed them 10th in their impressive World Championship debut.

When their longtime coaches retired in 2002, Dubreuil and Lauzon sold their house in Canada and moved to Lyon to train with coach Muriel Boucher-Zazoui. "It was hard to start over from scratch," Dubreuil says. "But now everything is at a higher technical level." The couple qualified for the Grand Prix Final for the third year in a row, but finished 10th again at 2003 Worlds.

Canadians | Saskatoon | January 2003

Born: August 11, 1974, Montreal, Quebec; November 26, 1975, Montreal

Hometown: Montreal

Training Site: Lyon, France

Coach: Muriel Boucher-Zazoui

Choreographer: Muriel Boucher-Zazoui

RESULTS

2001: 11th Worlds
6th Grand Prix Final
3rd Four Continents
2nd Sparkassen Cup
4th NHK

2002: 12th Olympics
10th Worlds
6th Grand Prix Final
2nd Skate Canada
4th Bofrost Cup

2003: 10th Worlds
4th Four Continents

Champions Series Final | Kitchener
December 2001

- Patrice started figure skating at nine, to improve his hockey skills. He played both sports until he was 14.

- Marie-France's mother didn't want her to start skating. So the resourceful girl asked her grandmother to buy her skates for her fifth birthday.

They feel they're ready for a big move upward. And from their experience at Canadian Nationals, they know they can do it.

Tatiana Navka & Roman Kostomarov

They were born in Moscow, they live in New Jersey, and they have represented Russia or Belarus with several previous partners ... including each other. Yes, Tatiana Navka and Roman Kostomarov do get around. And one of the places they are getting around to is the ice dancing podium at the World Championships. The veteran skaters came within one spot of the medals at the 2003 Worlds, by far their best finish ever. With anybody. Given ice dancing's resistance to quick change, their fourth-place finish in Washington was a gigantic leap from 2002, when the team had finished 10th at Olympics and eighth at Worlds.

Navka had been in the top 10 three times from 1993 to 1995, representing Belarus with Samuel Gezalian. But that partnership dissolved and she moved on to dance with Nikolai Morozov, with whom she finished 16th at the 1998 Olympics and 10th at Worlds. But that team split up too. Meanwhile, Kostomarov had won the World Junior Championship with Ekaterina Davydova in 1996, but by 1998 he, too, was searching for a new partner.

Navka and Kostomarov had complementary styles and lines, so they formed a new team, skating for coach Natalia Linichuk in Newark, Delaware. But despite a fairly successful first season together – third at Russian Nationals, 12th at 1999 Worlds – the chemistry wasn't working and the pair disbanded.

Kostomarov joined up with Anna Semenovich while Navka, without a skating partner, departed for Hackensack, New Jersey, to coach with her boyfriend, Alexander Zhulin. She and Zhulin got married, and in May of 2000 Navka gave birth to the couple's daughter, Sasha. Within a couple of weeks, Navka was back on the ice – teaching and training.

Kostomarov and his latest partner, Semenovich, finished second at Russian Nationals, 10th at Europeans and 13th at 2000 Worlds, but the pairing lasted only one season. In the spring, he called Navka and suggested that they were, after all, the most suitable partners for each other. She readily agreed. Her husband, the former world champion Zhulin, became their coach. And in 2001 Navka and Kostomarov re-emerged at Worlds with a 12th-place finish.

The couple's sweeping moves and strong footwork

Born: April 13, 1975, Dnepropetrovsk, Ukraine; Feburary 8, 1977, Moscow

Hometown: Moscow

Training Center: Hackensack, New Jersey

Coaches: Alexander Zhulin, Elena Tchaikovskaia

Choreographer: Tatiana Druchinina

RESULTS

2001: 12th Worlds
9th Europeans
4th Skate America
4th Cup of Russia

2002: 10th Olympics
8th Worlds
7th Europeans
2nd Cup of Russia
2nd Skate America

2003: 4th Worlds
2nd Grand Prix Final
3rd Europeans

Worlds | Washington | March 2003

served them well, and in each of the next two seasons they improved their standing by four places. They also won a silver medal at the prestigious Grand Prix Final in 2003. It might have taken them a lot of test driving, but it seems that Navka and Kostomarov are finally on the right road.

• Tatiana's role models when she was a young skater were ice dancing teams Torvill and Dean of England, and Russia's Usova and Zhulin. Alexander Zhulin eventually became her coach and husband.

Isabelle Delobel & Olivier Schoenfelder

Isabelle Delobel and Olivier Schoenfelder met during a training course in the French ice dance capital of Lyon, when they were just 12 years old.

It was 1990, a time of excitement and unlimited promise for the sport in their country. Isabelle and Paul Duchesnay had just won their second world medal, France's first podium placings in ice dance since 1962. Several other young French couples were on the rise. And the nucleus was Lyon, where the training course was being supervised by Russians Irina Moiseeva and Andrei Minenkov, the legendary "Min and Mo," one of the greatest dance teams in history.

Delobel and Schoenfelder had come to the camp with different partners, but Min and Mo liked the combination of a tall blond and the shorter brunette, and put them together. They've been together ever since. Delobel moved to Lyon from nearby Clermont-Ferrand, and Schoenfelder left his hometown of Belfort, near the Swiss border, so they could train with renowned dance teacher Lydie Bontems at the Lyon Ice Dance Centre.

With their classic but dynamic style, Delobel and Schoenfelder won silver at World Juniors in 1996. After

Born: June 17, 1978, Clermont-Ferrand, France; November 30, 1977, Belfort

Hometown: Lyon

Training Site: Lyon

Coach: Muriel Boucher-Zazoui

Choreographers: Margarita Drobiazko, Povilas Vanagas

RESULTS

2001: 13th Worlds
10th Europeans
3rd Skate Canada
5th Lalique Trophy

2002: 16th Olympics
12th Worlds
2nd Lalique Trophy
4th NHK

2003: 9th Worlds
7th Europeans
1st French Nationals

Worlds | Washington | March 2003

spending time in the United States with Tatiana Tarasova in 1999, they returned to Lyon to train under Muriel Boucher-Zazoui. In 2000 Delobel and Schoenfelder reached the podium at a Grand Prix event for the first time, winning bronze at Skate Canada.

With the retirement of Marina Anissina and Gwendal Peizerat, they won their first Senior Nationals in 2003, 13 years after they had formed a partnership. Discovering new approaches to lifts and edges by working with creative Lithuanians Margarita Drobiazko and Povilas Vanagas, Delobel and Schoenfelder cracked the top 10 at Worlds for the first time in 2003.

• Isabelle's twin sister, Veronique, also competes internationally in ice dance.

Worlds | Washington | March 2003

Kati Winkler & Rene Lohse

Although they both love ice dancing, Kati Winkler and Rene Lohse didn't choose figure skating. It chose them.

Winkler and Lohse grew up in the old nation of East Germany. When each of them was four years old, in kindergarten, Winkler and Lohse were identified as having athletic talent and were selected to be figure skaters.

They started in singles and had early successes, but neither was good at landing triple jumps. So, at 12, Lohse left skating and began playing soccer. Meanwhile, Winkler had back problems and had to stop singles skating in 1987. She was told she could switch to ice dancing, but there hadn't been any ice dance training in East Germany for 18 years. "I loved to skate and wanted to try it, but had no idea what to do," Winkler remembers. "So I started with some girls and we just had a book of rules. There were no boys."

Winkler remembered Lohse, who was in her class at school until 1985, and asked him to become her dance partner. He said yes.

"I was surprised, but I was yearning to skate again after two years," he says.

Since there was no ice dance coach, the new couple was assigned to Knut Schubert, a Berlin pairs coach. Other skaters laughed at them and said dancing wasn't a sport.

"But their minds changed quickly when they saw us work out of nothing and win the national junior title and go to two Junior World Championships," Lohse says.

The couple finished eighth at the 1992 World Juniors, but just as their career was blossoming, their country was united with West Germany. They had to work their way up through the ranks again. By 1996, Winkler and Lohse were German champions. That year, they moved from Berlin to Oberstdorf to work with coach Martin Skotnicky. They rose from 13th in the world in 1996 to sixth by 2000.

But then injuries began to strike. While riding his bike, Lohse was hit by a pickup truck and injured his shoulder. The team missed 2002 Europeans when he injured ligaments in

Born: January 16, 1974, Karl-Marx-Stadt, Germany; September 23, 1973, Berlin

Hometown: Berlin

Training Site: Oberstdorf

Coach: Martin Skotnicky

Choreographers: Kelly Johnson, Marc Bongaerts, Werner Lipowsky

RESULTS

2000: 6th Worlds
5th Europeans
3rd Lalique Trophy
4th Sparkassen Cup
3rd NHK

2001: 7th Worlds
5th Grand Prix Final
6th Europeans

2002: 8th Olympics
7th Worlds
3rd Bofrost Cup
4th Cup of Russia
2nd NHK

2003: 5th Europeans

Worlds | Nice | March 2000

• In the German army, Kati and Rene took basic training and attended seminars. Kati finished vocational training at Mercedes-Benz and Rene went to college – all while skating.

his knee. Winkler's flu forced them out of the 2003 Grand Prix Final, and muscle inflammation in Lohese's right leg kept them from 2003 Worlds. Their final Worlds before retirement are to be in 2004, in their Native Germany.

Megan Wing & Aaron Lowe

It's a good thing Megan Wing and Aaron Lowe are such an energetic couple, because they have to work hard for everything they get.

The veteran Canadian ice dance team has given so much to figure skating that it was gratifying to see them finally get something back in 2003. Although it was their 17th season together, it was just the second time that Wing and Lowe had qualified for the World Championships, and they found themselves knocking on the door of the top 10. Their 12th-place finish at their first Worlds since 2000 gave them optimism and reinforced their decision to remain in the sport until the 2006 Olympics. That will be a full 20 years after their partnership formed in Vancouver during 1986.

A couple off the ice as well as on it, Wing and Lowe have volunteered hundreds of hours of their time to various skating programs. In 2002–03, Wing was athlete representative to the Skate Canada board of directors and was a member of the National Teams Committee. Her partner is a member of the Skating Events Trust as well as athlete representative to the Canadian Olympic Council and AthletesCan. As if that weren't enough, they both attend the University of Windsor in Ontario.

Wing and Lowe have a smooth, refined skating style, which has matured even further since they switched training centers in 1999 from Montreal, where they spent more than a decade, to Detroit and highly regarded coach Igor Shpilband. The move paid off immediately with a bronze medal at the Sears Open. In 2002, they enjoyed a career highlight when they won the bronze at Four Continents, their first podium placing at a major ISU event.

Born: November 1, 1975, Vancouver, B.C.;
October 12, 1974, Vancouver

Hometown: Windsor, Ontario

Training Site: Detroit

Coaches: Igor Shpilband, Natalia Annenko

Choreographers: Igor Shpilband, Natalia Annenko

RESULTS

2000: 15th Worlds
4th Four Continents
2nd Canadian
Nationals
5th Skate Canada
7th Lalique Trophy

2001: 4th Four Continents
3rd Canadian
Nationals
6th Skate Canada
6th Skate America

2002: 3rd Four Continents
3rd Canadian
Nationals
6th Cup of Russia
6th NHK

2003: 12th Worlds
4th Four Continents
3rd Canadian
Nationals

Worlds | Washington | March 2003

If hard work has anything to do with it, it won't be their last.

• Megan severely damaged cartilage in her right knee two days before the freedance at 2003 Worlds and received 12 injections in the knee to help her complete the competition. "My partner is the strongest woman here," Aaron said.

Federica Faiella &
Massimo Scali

Ice dancing has been called a ladder that you can scale only a rung or two at a time. But Federica Faiella and Massimo Scali would like to take the climb a bit faster than that. The Winter Olympics return to Italy for the first time in 50 years, with Turin the host city in 2006.

The only Olympic figure skating medal ever won by Italy was the bronze at the 2002 Games by the wildly popular Barbara Fusar-Poli and Maurizio Margaglio. It was because of their famous countrymen that Faiella and Scali were able to get some baptism by fire at the 2002 Games in Salt Lake City. Because Fusar-Poli and Margaglio had won the 2001 world title, Italy had an extra ice dancing berth at Salt Lake City. Just a few days before the Games, the Italian federation decided to send their brand new team to the Olympics.

Their enthusiasm impressed the audiences in Salt Lake, but not the judges, who placed them 18th. But that wasn't a bad Olympic debut for a couple who had been together less than a year and whose female partner hadn't even completed her first full season of senior skating. Faiella and her former partner, Luciano Milo, finished second at Junior Worlds in 1998 and 1999, and they'd won a couple of national titles when Fusar-Poli and Margaglio didn't compete. But in the summer of 2000 Milo retired, ending their 10-year partnership. Meanwhile, Scali's partner, Flavia Ottaviani, had also retired.

By the autumn of 2001, Faiella and Scali had formed a new team and moved from Rome, and their close families, to Milan to train with coach Walter Rizzo. Because they

- Federica and Massimo are choreographed by Natalia Bestemianova and Andrei Bukin, the dramatic Russians who won four world titles and the 1988 Olympic ice dance championships.

Born: January 2, 1981, Rome;
November 12, 1979, Monterotondo

Hometown: Rome

Training Site: Milan

Coaches: Walter Rizzo, Brunhilde Bianchi

Choreographers: Natalia Bestemianova,
Andrei Bukin

RESULTS

2001: 2nd Nebelhorn Trophy
7th Skate Canada

2002: 18th Olympics
16th Worlds
12th Europeans
5th Skate Canada
5th Cup of Russia

2003: 11th Worlds
8th Europeans

Skate Canada | Quebec City | October 2002

receive no financial support from their federation, they have to pay their own way by choreographing young singles skaters for up to four hours a day. But the hard work soon started to pay off. When they finished eighth at the 2003 European Championships, it became clear that this was a team on the move. At the 2003 Worlds in Washington, Faiella and Scali improved seven places over the previous year to 11th.

Large jumps are harder to make the closer you are to the top 10, but with their own improvement and the retirements of other couples ahead of them, they could easily move up a few more spots by the time the Olympic season rolls around. Just in time, they hope, to challenge for a medal in Turin.

ACKNOWLEDGMENTS

To all the skaters, for providing such great inspiration over so many years.

To Firefly and the entire editorial and production team, including
Christine for design, and to Steve for delivering such good writing!

—*Gérard Châtaigneau*

Jessica and Toby, the perpetual muses.
Michelle who inspires everything.
June Burnside and:
Debbi Wilkes, Lois Elfman, Phil Hersh,
John Power, Mark Lund, Joyce Minten,
Paul Peret, Roland Zorn, Bev Smith, Shep Goldberg,
Marge Reynolds, Lori Nichol, Lorraine Quartaro.
And to Gérard, for his spectacular eye.

—*Steve Milton*